THE
COTTAGE GARDEN

COOL
SPRINGS
PRESS

CLAUS DALBY

Quarto.com

© 2023 Quarto Publishing Group USA Inc.
Text and photography © 2023 Claus Dalby, excepted as noted otherwise
The original Danish edition was published as:
Cottagehaver © Klematis A/S Denmark
(www.klematis.dk)

First Published in USA in 2023 by Cool Springs Press,
an imprint of The Quarto Group,
100 Cummings Center, Suite 265-D,
Beverly, MA 01915, USA.
T (978) 282-9590 F (978) 283-2742

Cool Springs Press titles are also available at discount for retail, wholesale, promotional, and bulk purchase. For details, contact the Special Sales Manager by email at specialsales@quarto.com or by mail at The Quarto Group, Attn: Special Sales Manager, 100 Cummings Center, Suite 265-D, Beverly, MA 01915, USA.

27 26 25 24 23   2 3 4 5

ISBN: 978-0-7603-7971-4

Digital edition published in 2023
eISBN: 978-0-7603-7972-1

Library of Congress Cataloging-in-Publication Data available

Design: Claus Dauby
Cover Image: Claus Dauby
Photography:Claus Dalby, unless otherwise noted
Translation: Tam McTurk, Citadel Translations, www.citadel.scot

Printed in China

Contents

Preface

I decided to write this book many years ago. It took quite a while to publish it for the simple reason that I had to make up my mind about which gardens to feature. And that took time—a lot of time.

Gardens with a real cottage feel aren't found on just any street corner, but I am happy with the many excellent examples that made their way into the book in the end. The search took me far and wide, but England is richly represented, of course. We start with Barnsdale Gardens, created by Geoff Hamilton (1936–1996), perhaps the most prominent figure in the recent cottage garden resurgence.

My journey also took me to Germany to an incredibly enchanting garden close to the Danish-German border. I titled this part of the book "The Real Thing" because this garden is one of the most cottage-like imaginable—not least due to its charming buildings.

My home country of Denmark is represented by three gardens. I made it to Sweden as well, specifically, to the picturesque little port of Kivik on the south coast. I also chose one garden in the United States. The book returns to England—the home of the style—in between each of these presentations from other countries.

The cottage garden is clearly more popular than ever, almost certainly because of its informal approach, the profusion of flowers, and the dreamy ambience. Of particular concern in our modern era, cottage gardens also offer great biodiversity. They are good places for human, animal, and insect life.

Claus Dalby

Foreword

Linda Vater

"Ask, and ye shall receive." For those of us longing for a garden book that captures the primal, simple, and loving essence of gardening, the universe has responded. The inimitable Danish gardener Claus Dalby gives us this beautiful book, *The Cottage Garden,* a classic interpretation of one of the most timeless and loved styles of gardening—the cottage garden. As Claus so simply and elegantly puts it, "it is because cottage gardens have a soul."

Here in *The Cottage Garden,* Claus captures, in pictures and words, the beautiful humility, charm, and—yes—soul, of these special places. Claus demystifies and interprets for us the qualities—horticultural, physical, and emotional—that make up the most compelling and evocative cottage gardens. By capturing incredible images of famous, iconic, and recognizable cottage gardens around the world, he gives us a glimpse into the artistry and magic of these cottage gardens' continuing appeal, and the imaginative minds of those who created them. This book captures the cultivated yet unrestrained wildness of these vibrant landscapes and the interwoven nature of their plant, human, animal, and insect inhabitants. In the pages of this book, the experiential sensibilities of the cottage garden, with all its buzzing, humming, climbing, and frolicking, jumps out at you and casts its spell.

By sharing the role of cottage gardens in the lives of those who tended them, and the rich medicinal and ornamental history of their place in the gardening realm, Claus explains the practical and artistic importance and untamed magic of cottage gardens. With his own keen eye and expertise in color, plant combinations, and the role of texture and light, Claus helps the reader translate the mysterious cottage garden formula into actionable ideas and insights for gardeners longing to capture the lovely simplicity and lifestyle of cottage gardening. Whether creating a cottage garden in the pastural countryside, a solitary garden bed of blooming shrubs, annuals, and perennials, or a modern interpretation of a cottage garden on a small hill in an urban neighborhood, this book is for you.

Linda Vater
Garden designer and lifestyle influencer,
author of *The Elegant and Edible Garden,* @potagerblog

Danish Garden History

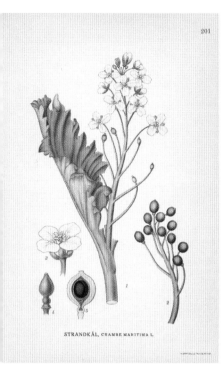

One plant the Vikings grew was sea kale, Crambe maritima. The illustration is from the ten-volume work Bildur ur Nordens Flora (Nordic Flora), published from 1901 until 1906, which was written and illustrated by the Swedish botanist Carl Axel Magnus Lindman.

My home country of Denmark may not have had a cottage tradition historically speaking, but cottage-style houses existed in the Romantic and Golden Ages, including during Hans Christian Andersen's lifetime (1805–1875). But let's start by looking further back to the first gardens in the country.

The First Gardens in Denmark

The first known kitchen gardens, apple orchards, and monastic gardens date from the Viking Age. Archaeological finds and written sources show that the Vikings grew curly kale, sea kale, ground elder, root vegetables, peas, and broad beans. Kitchen gardens were important, and it was said that "where there is a big garden, disease is rare." Curly kale, in particular, was a vitamin-rich ingredient in the winter diet.

The Vikings also used wild plants to season their food, including Nordic flora such as dill, juniper, cumin, mustard, wild garlic, and horseradish. Herbs that we now associate with more southerly climes were also grown in Denmark back then, including cilantro, marjoram, mint, and thyme.

Cloister and Apothecary Gardens

Cloister and apothecary gardens were widespread in the Middle Ages, when the main interest was in plants and herbs with healing properties, many of which also had beautiful flowers. A perfect example is the garden peony, *Paeonia officinalis*, which monks had brought to Denmark from southern Europe many years earlier.

The Danish medical writer Henrik Smid (approx. 1495–1563) recommended that women take dried common peony root in wine just after giving birth to bring on menstruation. It was also used to drive out kidney stones, cure jaundice, and alleviate stomach pains. From ancient times until a couple of hundred years ago, strings of peony seeds were hung around the necks of children with toothaches.

The common peony is fascinating because it became one of the best-known and best-loved flowers in peasant gardens. The beauty of its flowers was almost certainly the reason why the peony made the transition from cloister and apothecary gardens to ornamental ones.

Peasant Gardens

With the abolition of the Danish system of adscription (a successor to serfdom) in the late eighteenth century, peasants became free to own land and started to plant small gardens next to their newly built homes. The ruling classes and agricultural associations encouraged them to do so. The Royal Danish Agricultural Society (founded in 1769) sent a consultant around the country who planted gardens for these new farm owners and donated fruit trees and berry bushes.

They also planted willow trees for making fences (see the photo at the top of page 11) to keep animals out of their gardens and fields. Willow was particularly useful—it takes root easily, provides shelter, is used by thatchers and coopers, and can be used to make objects like maypoles, baskets, and brooms.

The purpose of the gardens was to help people become self-sufficient, so as well as fruit and berries, they grew vegetables and herbs. Thyme was said to be "one of the most distinguished herbs."

A beautiful house and fine garden with neatly pruned trees by the front door. People and animals line up for the photographer. Around 1880.

In Hans Christian Andersen's Day

"It was delightful out in the country: it was summer, and the corn fields were golden, the oats were green, the hay had been put up in stacks in the green meadows," wrote Hans Christian Andersen in *The Ugly Duckling* in 1843. It sounds beautiful and idyllic, just like the paintings from the Danish Golden Age (roughly 1800–1870).

The good, the true, and the beautiful were some of the themes addressed by Romanticism, but it was also a time of poverty and great economic hardship.

Before we head to England to learn about the cottage garden, I will end this section of the book with a verse from the song "Over Where the Road Makes a Turn," in which Andersen paints a bucolic portrait of a cottage:

Over where the road makes a turn
There lies a house so beautiful,
The walls stand a little crooked
The windows are very small
The door sags
The dog barks, that little creature,
Under the roof, swallows twitter,
The sun sets and so on.

A hardworking woman has taken her knitting outdoors. Note the fence. Around 1900.

An exceptionally pretty garden, with well-weeded and smoothly hoed paths, boxwood hedges and old, crooked fruit trees. Note the beehives. The bees pollinated fruit and berries and provided honey for the pantry. Around 1900.

An elderly couple by the roses in front of their home. Around 1900.

The English Cottage Garden

English garden culture has been well documented, with myriad accounts of the many large and impressive gardens on big estates and castle grounds. The colorful descriptions and plans, some hundreds of years old, reveal the scale of these gardens and the skill involved in designing them. Great works have been written about them too.

One particular chapter in English garden history that is not as well documented, but is just as interesting, is the cottage garden. With their uncultivated aesthetic and picturesque charm, cottage gardens encapsulate the spirit of the English countryside beloved by so many. They speak to us of an idyllic past.

Everybody with even the slightest Anglophile streak is fascinated by Jane Austen's (1775–1817) expressive descriptions of nineteenth-century England. Despite focusing on the upper classes, her stories also depict a plethora of minor characters, and the period settings are so vividly portrayed that it's like being there yourself.

England is beautiful, and I visit gardens there at least once a year. There are always new ones to explore.

Among other things, the Great Dixter Gardens are known for their beautiful flowering meadows.

The Great Dixter Gardens, in the south of England, were created by gardener and author Christopher Lloyd (1921–2006). Not only was this his childhood home, but also he lived there until his death. In 1909, Lloyd's parents bought the beautiful old house, which was built in the Middle Ages. Now it is open to the public.

Helen Allingham

Helen Allingham (1848–1926) had a penchant for small, picturesque places. Her watercolors are a beautiful testimony to a bygone age. The paintings on the next page are from the book *The Victorian World of Helen Allingham*.

There are many old photographs of English gardens, but their focus was usually on estates and stately homes. Few photographers cared about the rural poor.

Fortunately, some painters were fascinated by subjects and motifs that were a little off the beaten track. One of them was Helen Allingham (1848–1926). You can almost smell the flowers and hear the birds singing in her paintings.

Allingham was one of the most prominent late-nineteenth-century artists to depict cottage gardens. Born into an artistic family, she attended the Royal Academy of Arts in London in 1867. Several years later, she met the poet William Allingham (1824–1889), and although he was somewhat older, they married in 1874. They lived a happy, artistically fulfilling life together until his death fifteen years later. After her husband's death, Allingham painted full-time, something she had not done for years.

She was from Surrey in the south of England, a place that informed the motifs for the paintings that made her so famous and beloved. Her work conveys the character of local settings in a uniquely empathetic manner. She had a remarkable ability to capture an elder bush in bloom, a group of delphiniums, or scattered foxgloves in just a few brush strokes.

Allingham illustrated many books, including the classic *Happy England*, first published in 1903. Time seemed to stand still in her paintings, although some people find them overly idyllic. They also represented the diametric opposite of the Industrial Revolution that transformed English cities from the mid-eighteenth century onward. Industrialization called for extra labor, and many people moved from the countryside to the cities. These workers didn't become rich, though—far from it. They usually ended up living in slums, where the more well-to-do never set foot. The growing working class lived wretched lives under poor conditions, in unhealthy, damp homes surrounded by open sewers.

Poverty was also commonplace in the countryside, but at least the rural poor had access to natural light and clean air. It's little wonder so many people liked Allingham's work—and still do. Her paintings and those of her peers (e.g., Myles Birket Foster, 1825–1899) echo something deeply rooted in the English soul.

Helen Allingham 15

William Robinson

William Robinson (1838–1935) was ahead of his time. He challenged the Victorian era's rigid, artificial flower beds, encouraging wild planting instead.

The Irish gardener and author William Robinson (1838–1935) was an ardent admirer of cottage gardens and often mentioned them in his articles and books. He was a pioneer, the first prominent public advocate for wild gardening. He rejected Victorian parterre beds, neatly arranged summer flowers in bright colors, and species like jewelweed, sage, ice begonia, carnations, and marigolds, as well as tropical and subtropical plants grown in greenhouses.

Robinson notoriously described a flower bed in the Royal Horticultural Society's garden in Kensington as "false and ugly." His comment caused quite a stir. So zealous was his crusade for wildflowers that some suggested he was possessed by the devil.

Robinson's first book, *Gleanings from French Gardens*, was published in 1868. More followed, including his best-known work, *The Wild Garden*, in 1870. In it, he wrote, "What is more beautiful than to see the winter aconite flowering under a grove of naked trees in February and later disappear when the grass begins to grow. Or snowdrops growing in the grass in a clearing in the woods!"

He introduced the principle of planting bulbs, such as daffodils, in the grass and letting them grow there. He also advocated planting perennials in grass: "Many perennials are too strong and unruly to make the most of the traditional perennial bed. But planted in grass, they are held back so much that they do not spread unchecked, and here it is of little import that the flowering time is short. Good examples include Japanese knotweed, Solomon's seal, meadow cranesbill, comfrey, white hellebore, barrenwort, galega, ligularia and peonies, and most of these plants are distinguished by their leaves."

Robinson also hailed the living hedge as one of the English countryside's most distinctive features: "Exceedingly important are hawthorn and holly, which make hedgerows impenetrable. As a supplement, wild roses, ivy, clematis, honeysuckle, and sloe will adorn hedges all year round."

The Wild Garden was reprinted again and again, in eight different editions, until 1932. The final edition was an expanded edition printed in 2009 by Timber Press and was still available at the time of this writing.

In 1871, Robinson also began publishing weekly papers, first *The Garden* and later *Gardening Illustrated*.

He was a diligent writer and skilled businessman. In 1883, he published *The English Flower Garden*, a book that made him the most famous gardener in the country. Again, with no holds barred, he launched a broadside against large, tiled gardens and their parterre beds while singing the praises of the cottage garden, which flourished for nine months a year and was humanity's finest achievement.

Business was booming, and Robinson prospered. In 1885, he bought Gravetye Manor in Sussex and planted trees and shrubs on the grounds. Around the house, he grew sizable areas of scillas, cyclamen, and other spring flowers in between hazel bushes and chestnut trees. Along the forest edges and in clearings, he planted daffodil bulbs by the thousands, along with robust perennials. Other projects included a huge, round, walled kitchen garden, a heather garden, and a water garden.

Gravetye is still a fine garden. It is now home to a luxury hotel with a gourmet restaurant supplied by the kitchen garden Robinson established over a century ago.

You can follow @gravetyemanor on Instagram.

Purchased by William Robinson in 1885, Gravetye Manor is now a hotel. It employs several gardeners to tend to its awe-inspiring grounds.

Gertrude Jekyll

Gertrude Jekyll (1843–1932) was a pioneer. These hand-colored photographs clearly show that she had an excellent eye for shape and color when composing beds. The pictures are of her own garden, Munstead Wood, in 1912.

Another prominent figure in English garden history is the designer, artist, and author Gertrude Jekyll (1843–1932), who designed several hundred gardens and was famous for the way she mixed plants and focused on their shapes and colors.

Jekyll was fascinated by the plants and flowers from her childhood. A governess gave her what would become her favorite book, *Flowers of the Field*, which she read over and over until she wore it out and had to get a new copy—twice. The young Gertrude was particularly interested in languages, music, and art, and spent a great deal of time embroidering, drawing, and painting. At seventeen, she started a two-year course at South Kensington School of Art.

Her studies were greatly influenced by her childhood interest in flowers and plants. In 1875, she met William Robinson. Jekyll was deeply fascinated by Robinson and his ideas and frequently referred to *The Wild Garden* when helping her mother design and plant gardens, an activity that also allowed her to explore her creative side. For his part, Robinson was fascinated by her perspective on plants. Their meeting was the start of a close, fifty-year friendship.

Over time, Robinson realized that Jekyll was also quite the writer and had plenty of interesting insights to share. He hired her to write for his magazines, and she made her debut in 1881. Over the years, she penned more than a thousand articles.

In 1899, Jekyll published her first book, *Wood and Garden*, in which she wrote, "I have learnt much from the little cottage gardens that help to make our English waysides the prettiest in the whole temperate world. One can hardly go into the smallest cottage garden without learning or observing something new. It may be some two plants growing beautifully together by some happy chance, or a pretty mixed tangle of creepers, or something that one always thought must have a south wall doing better on an east one."

Jekyll lived in Surrey and loved to go riding on a little pony cart. She would drive along narrow roads, enjoying the lush cottage gardens, talking to gardeners and perhaps taking home a few cuttings. She may even have passed some of the beautiful places and gardens Helen Allingham painted during the same period. Who knows?

Vita Sackville-West

Vita Sackville-West (1892–1962) and her husband, Harold Nicolson (1886–1968), designed one of the world's most famous gardens–Sissinghurst Castle Garden. The photograph shows them in front of South Cottage.

The English poet and author Vita Sackville-West (1892–1962) is another well-known horticulturist who derived great joy and inspiration from the cottage garden. Her place in garden history was guaranteed when she and her husband–author, politician, and diplomat Harold Nicolson (1886–1968)–created Sissinghurst Castle Garden in Kent.

When they bought the property in 1930, it was so dilapidated that it would be years before they moved in. In the meantime, they started work on the garden that would become one of the most famous in the world. Her fame is also partly attributable to her affair with well-known author Virginia Woolf (1882–1941).

Back then, the gardening world was small. In 1917, Sackville-West and her mother visited Gertrude Jekyll. By that time, Vita had developed a deep interest in gardening and had read several of Jekyll's books. She also crossed paths with William Robinson. In 1927, after reading her poem "The Land," he sent her a letter praising it and inviting her to Gravetye Manor. Sackville-West accepted and rode the approximately 19 miles (30 km) to visit the famous gardener.

Sackville-West later recounted how these two great pioneers helped shape her gardening life. She was particularly fascinated by William Robinson's books *The Wild Garden* and *The English Flower Garden*.

Sissinghurst Castle Garden began to take shape in the 1930s. Nicolson had a keen eye and drew up a plan that divided the garden into areas of different sizes enclosed by hedges and walls. He also enlisted the aid of the architect Albert Reginald Powys (1881–1936), who specialized in preserving buildings. They made an effective team and devised a well-thought-out design that still works today.

Several buildings, which had mostly been used for agricultural purposes, were demolished. Otherwise, of course, it was a matter of preserving as much as possible, including the lovely little South Cottage, some distance from the rest of the buildings. The restored dwelling incorporated a bedroom for Sackville-West and a study and library for Nicolson.

The property also included a space enclosed by hedges known as the Cottage Garden or the Sunset Garden. The red, orange, and yellow color scheme resembled a fiery sunset, something of a departure from the pastel palette of the typical cottage garden.

Sackville-West loved the garden and described it as "sea of flowers with winding passages, probably the nicest type of small garden that England has ever produced."

In the late 1930s, Sissinghurst Castle Garden opened to the public and has remained so ever since. Sackville-West died in 1962. The year before his death in 1968, Nicolson donated Sissinghurst (as the property is commonly known) to the National Trust.

South Cottage opened to the public for the first time in 2017, and guided tours now provide insight into the famous couple's life.

Even though Sackville-West saw the garden at South Cottage as her own, it was and still is open to the public.

Margery Fish

Margery Fish (1892–1969) in the garden at East Lambrook Manor, one of the most authentic cottage gardens of recent times.

The last of the great English garden ladies I wish to present here is Margery Fish (1892–1969), a writer whose books provide perhaps the most in-depth treatment of the cottage garden and its flowers.

Fish was deeply committed to selecting and cultivating plants once common in rural gardens. She was an incredibly diligent writer and author and shared her knowledge in numerous books and articles. One of her most popular books, *Cottage Garden Flowers*, is still in print.

In it, she writes, "Nowhere in the world is there anything quite like the English cottage garden. In every village and hamlet in the land, there were these little gardens, always gay, and never garish and so obviously loved. There are not so many now, alas, of those cottages of cob or brick, with their thatched roofs and tiny crooked windows, [. . .] but the flowers remain, that have come to be known as 'cottage flowers' because of their simple, steadfast properties."

Fish moved in 1932 to East Lambrook Manor in Somerset, where her garden is still open to the public. It has been maintained by a succession of new owners over the years.

The many distinctive features of Fish's gardening include an extravagant style and dense planting. "Plants are friendly creatures and enjoy each other's company. The close-packed plants in a cottage garden grow well and look happy," she stated. No wonder then that she was a prominent advocate of ground-covering plants such as cranesbill.

However, her favorite plants were primroses and auriculae, and her garden was home to over sixty wild and bred varieties, many of which she sold in her nursery. Lungwort was another favorite, mainly because of the early flowers in bluish, purple, pink, and white. Her writings also often celebrated foliage—she was incredibly fond of columbine. Her penchant for snowdrops is evident, too, as she had more than fifty different varieties.

Fish's books are packed full of good advice, and she focused on three points in particular: The first was the importance of the colors of the plants—not just the flowers but also the foliage and seedheads. Second, she liked to choose good neighbors—plants that thrive side by side and don't suffocate each other. She also advocated planting in the right place so that the plants enjoyed the right growth conditions—for example, sun or shade, moist or well-drained, clay-rich or calcareous soil.

Stephen Lacey, a longstanding columnist for the *Telegraph* wrote about East Lambrook Manor:

Uneven, winding paths filled with self-seeded plants lead the visitor through the garden, which is filled with primroses, cranesbill, hollyhocks, bell flowers, masterwort, lungwort, spurge, columbine and Christmas roses. Occasionally, you encounter vegetables side by side with shrubs, classic English perennials and rare plants from the East. Roses and honeysuckle beside apple trees, and the house and barn are almost engulfed in foliage. Here, there are no long vistas, so what constantly preoccupies the mind and eye is all the many plants covering the ground around your feet. And that is what makes it such a wonderful experience!

At East Lambrook Manor, new and old are blended in a relaxed, informal way, resulting in a garden full of grace and charm.

A beautifully colorful array of candelabra primulas. Primulas were Fish's favorite plants.

Tasha Tudor

For well over a quarter of a century, I have visited and photographed hundreds of beautiful gardens, each more stunning than the last. I am fortunate, not only as a photographer and author but also as a garden enthusiast, to have visited some extremely beautiful places. This book bears witness to my good fortune, and I'm delighted and proud of the selection of gardens in it.

However, there is one garden I would very much like to have included. It would have been the crowning glory. But it wasn't possible, for an all-too-sad reason—the owner is no longer with us, and I feel that I would not have been able to do her masterpiece justice without first hearing her describe the thinking behind it.

The garden in question was the brainchild of American children's book author and illustrator Tasha Tudor (1915–2008). She lived in Vermont, a little over 300 miles (480 km) north of Boston. Like so many other garden lovers, I know of her garden because of *Tasha Tudor's Garden*. Published in the United States in 1994, the book celebrates her incredibly poetic cottage garden. I stumbled across it in a bookstore in London shortly after it was published and found myself deeply fascinated by Tudor's universe. Thousands of readers worldwide must feel the same, as the book has been a tremendous success.

Back then, in the mid- to late1990s, I was not internet savvy. These days, I would just have dashed off an email asking if I could visit Tasha and her garden. I often thought about sending a letter but never got around to it. For some reason, I didn't think about the fact that she had been born in 1915.

In 2008, I read her obituary online. She passed away peacefully, aged ninety-two, in her beautiful old cottage in the middle of the enchanting garden, surrounded by friends and family, as well as her beloved Welsh corgis, who always followed her around the garden.

Even the *New York Times* published an extensive obituary. Tudor was a big name in the English-speaking world, especially in the United States. Several have called her the United States' answer to England's Beatrix Potter (1866–1943). Her first book was published in 1938, and she wrote and illustrated over a hundred others, which focused mainly on her own nostalgic milieu and dogs.

Tudor was particularly popular in Japan, and just before her death, a Japanese film crew recorded a short film about her. It's available on YouTube (search for "Tasha Tudor's Garden").

I was so disappointed that I never got to meet Tasha Tudor that I decided to publish her book in Danish. It took some time to obtain the rights, but in 2011 my own publisher, Klematis, published *Tasha Tudors Have*. Søren Ryge Petersen reviewed it in the Danish newspaper *Politiken*:

> The pictures by Richard W. Brown, in particular, are a constant delight because not a single one is superfluous or immaterial, and because many are so beautiful, you feel transported to the masterpieces of the Golden Age painters. Rarely has the boundary between photography and painting been as fluid as here, which is no coincidence, of course, because Tasha Tudor spent much of her time drawing and painting and always used her garden as a motif.

> She is a legend in the United States because she infuses life into one of the enduring American dreams: the simple, beautiful, frugal life in the little house on the prairie. Not an everyday life and battle for survival, but the time of life when you are a grandparent and can do whatever you want.

There is no doubt in my mind that William Robinson would have loved Tudor's garden.

A couple of pages from
Tovah Martin's book about
Tasha Tudor. Richard
W. Brown's captivating
photos beautifully convey
her garden's fairy-tale
atmosphere.

Tasha Tudor wanted to live near her son in a lovely, old wooden house with a beautiful garden outside. Her son built the house, and Tasha established and cared for the garden. She seems to have been a devout, moral person and a lifelong wearer of home-knitted garments.

Her family lineage may well be from England because the garden is unmistakably in the English cottage style, with big, mixed perennial beds and an exquisite sense of color. Add two dogs, a parrot and a herd of goats, and the scene is set for a fairy story that might have taken place 150 years ago but actually unfolded in Vermont on the eastern seaboard just two decades ago.

I still wanted to learn more about Tasha Tudor. My chance came when I visited New England in 2015. A mutual garden friend put me in touch with Tovah Martin, the author of *Tasha Tudor's Garden*.

I really looked forward to meeting her, and we spent a couple of pleasant days in each other's company, visiting several beautiful gardens. Traveling between the far-flung gardens left us plenty of time to talk. There was so much I wanted to know about Tudor, and I asked Tovah all sorts of questions.

She had a lot of good things to say. As well as being sweet and friendly, Tudor was apparently also very genuine. She really did dress as if she was from another century. Her garden was utterly enchanting all year round—the pictures I'd seen were in no way manipulated. Tasha Tudor truly was Tasha Tudor!

We also talked about English garden culture, touching on William Robinson at one point. Tovah mentioned that one of Tudor's bibles was Robinson's famous book, *The Wild Garden*. It made perfect sense. I am absolutely sure that Robinson would have loved her garden.

Cottage Garden Inspiration

Creative cottage-style wickerwork supporting dahlias.

Why are cottage gardens so widely admired and coveted? I'm pretty sure it's because they have a soul. We are drawn to the lush, the informal, the slightly wild. It's a haphazard approach to gardening, in which empty spaces are banned. Plants are tightly packed, shoulder to shoulder. It's about being deliberately wild.

My own garden is far from the cottage style, but I am greatly inspired by it. I have drawn on the best from many eras: tight yew hedges from the Baroque garden, pruned trees from the Renaissance garden, winding paths and a garden pavilion from the English garden, and plants from the cottage garden. My garden pays homage to the natural world and is inspired by both William Robinson's and Margery Fish's books.

Within the overall framework, I like to use plants that look wild, for example, the kinds of umbelliferous plants we often see at the edge of ditches. I particularly like cow parsley and wild carrot, the latter of which is also poetically named Queen Anne's lace by the English. Dill and fennel, with their lime-colored inflorescences, are also important elements in my beds.

My Dutch friend Marieke Nolsen is a floral artist with the most amazing little cottage garden.

As the pictures in this book show, some of the most cottage-like flowers are annuals and biennials that I propagate from seeds, but then go on to self-seed.

The annuals include pansy, poppy, snapdragon, and sweet pea. Alongside the umbelliferous plants, the biennials play a considerable role in establishing the character of the garden—especially forget-me-not, silver dollar, dame's violet, and foxglove.

Perennials are also important, and I use some of the most well-known and traditional plants, such as columbine, primroses, masterwort, cranesbill, hollyhocks, delphinium, bellflower, peony, carnation, knapweed, marguerites, foxglove, and lupins. The finishing touches come from rose, honeysuckle, and clematis. Berry bushes, fruit trees, dahlias, and vegetables also coexist in perfect harmony here.

Cottage gardens of the past would typically also have had animals, perhaps a couple of pigs and maybe a cow. That would be less practical these days, of course, but beehives, birdhouses, and insect hotels are common features of the modern cottage garden. If you have the space and courage to keep chickens, pigeons, and/or ducks, it's just a matter of getting on with it.

You can also add to the cottage atmosphere with charming, decorative, and practical features—old garden tools, mini greenhouses, patinated pots and jars, zinc buckets, wicker baskets, glass-covered frames, wickerwork, chestnut fences, gates, and smaller sheds.

If you want to know more about English gardens, I highly recommend Ursula Buchan's excellent and inspiring book *The English Garden*.

Every year, Marieke starts all over again, pre-cultivating dahlias, sowing summer flowers, and planting bulbs. It's a dense flower universe. Follow @mariekenolsen on Instagram.

The People's Gardener

One of the biggest champions of cottage gardens more recently was the well-known British TV personality Geoff Hamilton (1936–1996). From 1979 until his death in 1996, he hosted *Gardeners' World* on the BBC.

First aired in 1968, *Gardeners' World* remains one of the BBC's most enduring programs more than fifty years later. Hamilton joined the team in 1975 and took over as the main host four years later.

He was well known and loved for his relaxed approach to gardening. When he died of a heart attack at just fifty-nine, the English garden world was plunged into mourning. It was not without reason that he was called "the people's gardener." His calm and quietly informative manner held universal appeal.

Hamilton developed an interest in gardening at an early age, and in his spare time, he worked at local nurseries on the outskirts of London, where he grew up. In 1959, he graduated from the esteemed Writtle Agricultural College in Essex, after which he opened the Hamilton Garden Centre in Northamptonshire. He was passionate about organic horticulture and wrote articles about it long before it became a familiar and widespread concept.

In 1983, Hamilton and his family bought a small farm in South Yorkshire, close to Barnsdale Forest. The garden center was no more. He had long wanted to find a place to start a garden from scratch. After searching for a while, he found a suitable plot of about five acres, the future site of his dream project—Barnsdale Gardens. It may have started out as bare earth, but the gardens soon started to take shape. In the mid-eighties, Barnsdale Gardens became the focal point of *Gardeners' World*, and viewers were enthralled by the many different small spaces—not least, the Gentleman's Cottage Garden.

Hamilton was a highly accomplished plantsman, but he also possessed numerous other hands-on skills and was often filmed making items such as sheds, furniture, frames, gates, and fences. His small structures were always a perfect fit for the cottage garden. His book *Geoff Hamilton's Cottage Gardens* includes working drawings for several of his DIY projects (see pages 36–37).

Crucially, Hamilton made sure that all his minor projects, be it planting or building, were affordable. He showed how to grow plants from seeds and cuttings and used various recycled materials to achieve a proper "cottage look."

After his death in 1996, his son Nick took over Barnsdale Gardens, which remains open to the public. Nick inherited his father's passion for the simple cottage garden style. For more than a decade, he has been president of the Cottage Garden Society, which works to promote and preserve these unique places.

Barnsdale Gardens is particularly popular with the older generation, who recognize

many of its features from *Gardeners' World*. As you walk around, you can't help but notice that many of the guests are still talking about Hamilton. Viewers clearly loved him. Several old clips with him are available online, as is the BBC documentary *Geoff Hamilton: A Man and His Garden*. At the start, he is making the wooden archway in the picture above.

If you want to see more of Hamilton, I recommend the DVD box set *The Geoff Hamilton BBC Collection*, which contains three DVDs. One of them is just about cottage gardens.

Barnsdale Gardens is a remarkably inspiring place, with no fewer than thirty-eight separate spaces arranged like pearls on a string. The layout is wonderfully enchanting—creating different moods in different parts of the gardens was perhaps Hamilton's greatest skill.

◄ Peonies are a must in the cottage garden. Although they look incredibly delicate, they are among the hardiest perennials. In a suitable spot—preferably clay-rich, moist, and in full sun—they will come back year after year. This one is the best known and most popular variety, 'Sarah Bernhardt'. You will never go wrong with her!

As for the plants themselves, they are mostly well-known varieties, for which Hamilton was a prominent advocate. He made good use of robust and reliable plants. Many of them are on sale in Barnsdale's well-stocked nursery.

Hamilton often recommended the peony not only for its sumptuous flowers but also because of the beautifully captivating shoots that emerge in the spring.

▶ Many people are particularly keen on double peonies because their full flowers ooze romance and pastoral idyll. Personally, I am deeply fond of the single-flowering ones, which are less prone to falling over and have exposed, vibrating stamens that bees love—a bit like a bee magnet.

▲ I can't be certain, but I am pretty sure Hamilton featured the beautiful climbing rose 'Constance Spry' in bloom several times. It is absolutely breathtaking, with large spherical flowers that look almost like peony heads.

▶ No cottage garden is complete without foxglove, or digitalis. This one is 'Sutton's Apricot'. Foxgloves come in an incredible range of colors, but this apricot-hued variety is particularly popular.

▲ Another of Hamilton's favorites was cranesbill, which comes in multiple varieties and sizes. Many are in shades of pink, while the white ones are a little rarer. This beautiful variety is called *Geranium sanguineum* 'Album'.

◄ Another lovely pink peony. This beauty is called 'Dr Alexander Fleming'.

▼ The picture below shows how peonies form a large cluster. It is clear that these have been there for some years.

Hamilton wrote several books, one of which I have previously mentioned—*Geoff Hamilton's Cottage Gardens*. It was published in 1995, the year before his death, and has been reprinted several times. It is currently out of print, but copies are often available at reasonable prices from secondhand booksellers, including online.

◀ ▲ The book contains working drawings for many of the DIY projects Hamilton shared on TV. They are still there in Barnsdale Gardens, all in his signature gray-blue shade. He called this piece the love bench.

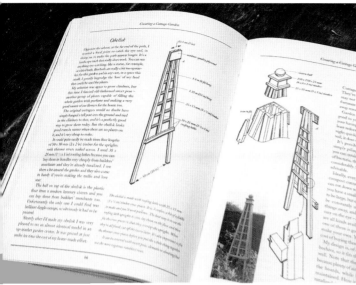

▲ ▶ Geoff Hamilton's DIY construction projects are beautifully made and well proportioned, with a classic feel. His designs have spread beyond Barnsdale Gardens. Over the years, I have seen many obelisks similar to this one. It makes a fantastic focal point in any garden.

Watching Hamilton working with wood in his TV programs, you couldn't help but be swept along by his enthusiasm when he talked about how cheaply he had made this or that. For example, he was clearly delighted to tell viewers that the top of the obelisk was made of the floating ball from a toilet cistern.

"Cheap and cheerful" was almost a mantra for Hamilton. His mission was to share the joy of gardening, something he found incredibly rewarding, with everyone—even those for whom money was tight.

◀ This is Hamilton's arch, a portal or entranceway from one part of the gardens to another. Google "garden arch" and marvel at the vast array of imaginative constructions, some of which are more striking than pretty. But with its simple construction, Hamilton's arch is refined and unpretentious, making it the perfect fit for a cottage garden. Several drawings of it appear in *Geoff Hamilton's Cottage Gardens*.

Hamilton's timeless, homemade carpentry is an inspiration to pick up a hammer and saw, perhaps to make this plant rack, which can be freestanding or suspended (as shown here).

Hamilton called it an auriculae theater, a fairly well-known concept in the English gardening world. These theaters—which, as the name suggests, were used for exhibiting auriculae—were highly popular in the Victorian era. At that time, they often had a rococo-inspired style, far removed from the cottage garden aesthetic. However, Hamilton liked the idea so much that he developed this version—and instead of auriculae, geraniums were the stars in his theater.

▶ Plastic furniture had already started making inroads into English gardens in Hamilton's day. Needless to say, he felt the material didn't fit the cottage style. He was ahead of his time, a pioneer in organic horticulture, who sang the virtues of wildlife-friendly gardens and was very much in favor of recycling and DIY. He left an indelible mark on the English garden world. It is sad that he left us so soon, as he would undoubtedly have appealed to an entirely new generation of gardeners.

◀ Roses are a must in a cottage garden. This is the David Austin rose 'Scepter'd Isle'. The delicate scent and goblet-shaped flowers make it a fantastic fit for a romantic garden setting.

▼ The swathes of flowers in this illustration from *Geoff Hamilton's Cottage Gardens* epitomize his idea of the perfect cottage garden.

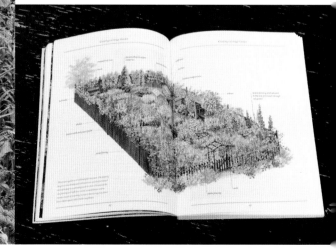

The Real Thing

When I first visited this charming property in Schleswig-Holstein, Germany, in about 2015, it really fired up my enthusiasm, not only for the garden but also for the whole farm. Located in the small town of Hestoft, this place is over two hundred years old and has a truly authentic cottage garden ambience.

The name of the area reveals that it used to be part of Denmark. The suffix "toft" stems from a Danish term for a fenced-in plot of land. Here, it means a horse paddock.

Some friends recommended Hestoft when I first floated the idea of a book about cottage gardens. They had heard about it while on a cycling holiday in this reagion. I contacted the owners of the farm, told them about the book project, and was warmly welcomed.

Heidi and Michael Chalupka purchased the farm in 1993. Initially, it was mainly the buildings they found enchanting. They had spent years searching for a place with soul and charm, and this was it—or, more precisely, this was where they could eventually make their dreams come true, with a bit of hard work. The farm was in dire need of tender loving care, but Heidi and Michael (an architect) were undeterred. They had been looking for something unspoiled to restore. People working in museums often say that poverty preserves. The buildings retained many of their original features, but they had all been badly neglected, and the new owners had to act fast.

The garden, too, was in a sad state, mainly consisting of nettles, thickets, elder bushes, and wild undergrowth. But Heidi and Michael saw the site's potential and emphasized the positive; for example, the old fruit trees just needed some gentle pruning.

At first, the couple concentrated on the house. Seven years later, in 2000, it was ready for them to move in. By then, they had replaced most of the brickwork and timber, including the frame, and most of the rafters and beams. They also rethatched the roof. Much of the time had been taken up with sourcing materials that suited the buildings' character.

Various small structures, including a hen house, are scattered around the site. They may look as if they were built at the same time as the farm, but they are all Michael's work, based on traditional designs he studied in living history museums.

Heidi and Michael are both interested in history and collect old agricultural tools and artifacts. Over the years, their collection grew so big that they opened a little museum at one end of the farmyard.

Today, the fully restored farm complex is a wonderfully coherent whole. The captivating garden, with its traditional farm flora, crooked trees, and cozy seating areas makes this a lovely destination for excursions, attracting visitors from far and wide.

▲ In early spring (in this photo, April), you can clearly see the layout of the garden. Inspired by old farm gardens, it is bordered by gravel paths that wind around the beds. The trunks and branches of the fruit trees add life and character and create a memorable, welcoming atmosphere. Michael made the toolshed from recycled materials. Small outbuildings are always a charming addition to any garden, helping create different spaces and adding rustic flavor. The low rows of sticks along the edges of the beds are made of hazel. Willow is also an option, but hazel lasts longer.

◀ The drumstick primrose (*Primula denticulate*), 'Alba', is a delicate, discreet little bloom and a perfect fit for this garden. It is a relatively short-lived plant that thrives in moist and slightly shaded areas, as do most primroses.

▲ Traditionally, herbs were an important part of farm gardens. Older locals tell me that there used to be a large kitchen garden here. Growing herbs is Heidi's domain, and these days she makes do with a relatively small plot surrounded by a chestnut fence. The white fabric protects newly planted lettuce from frost.

▶ I have not been able to determine the name of this beautiful yellow daffodil with the orange corona. It was here when the couple moved in. Over the years, they have divided the groups and replanted the bulbs, one by one, roughly 4 inches (10 cm) apart. That way, they flower again and again. If the bulbs cluster too closely together, they eventually only produce leaves—no flowers. Small tulips also grew in the garden when the couple took it over (see the photo on pages 40–41).

△ Michael and Heidi have laid fine pea gravel on the paths. You can just spread gravel directly on the soil, but the result is more durable if you remove the top 4 inches (10 cm) or so of soil, spread the gravel, pack it down, and add approximately 2.5 inches (5 cm) of more gravel.

◁ Old farmhouse gardens rarely had lawns. They were far more common in the more "sophisticated" gardens at castles and manor houses. Grass belonged to meadows and fields, and the farmer usually cut it with a scythe— as does Michael in the meadow at the end of the garden. Many wildflowers blossom here in summer, including poppies and cornflowers (see page 60). Closer to the house, Michael and Heidi use a lawnmower to keep the grass at an appropriate length. As fans of the natural look, they only mow it a couple of times a month.

▷ A group of small bantam chickens live in the garden. They not only lay eggs but also remove weeds and supply fertilizer. The breed, called Chabo, is native to Japan, which is why they are also sometimes called Japanese dwarf chickens. They first came to England in the 1860s and arrived in the United States a few years later. According to Michael, a significant number were imported into Germany around 1870 and have been bred there ever since.

▲ It's hard to imagine a more charming hen house. The hens have no designated space of their own but spend all day meandering around the garden and meadow before being shut in for the night. Out here in the countryside, the rooster is free to crow as loudly as he wishes!

▶ This drumstick primrose (*Primula denticulata*) is violet. There is also a burgundy variant. To make sure it grows again, divide the green leaf rosettes, which increase in number every year. Plant them individually, and they will multiply again next year. Soon you will have plenty of them.

▲ The couple allows the grass in the meadow by the garden to grow until late summer before cutting it with a scythe. Michael does use the lawnmower from time to time during the summer, and the contrast between the cut and uncut grass is pleasing to the eye, especially when the uncut grass is quite long.

◄ ▶ The farm is next to open fields where the neighbor's cows and sheep graze. Heidi and Michael only have chickens and a single cat, but in the olden days, cows and pigs were also kept at the farm. The old stable is now a museum, and much of the arable land has been sold off.

▶ Clematis comes in all sizes and in varieties that flower at all points of the growing season. *Clematis alpina* 'Ruby' produces purple flowers in May. Some people find clematis challenging to grow, but it's really quite simple. Given a chance, it grows quite happily, so here are a few tips: When planting, dig a hole slightly larger than the plant's container. Immerse the pot with the clematis in water so that the soil is well soaked. Mix garden soil with compost or good potting soil and fill the bottom of the hole. If you have an old pillow with down that you are willing to sacrifice, slash it open and mix the down with the soil in the hole. As they decompose, the feathers will turn into fertilizer. Deposit the plant in the hole so that the upper edge of the pot is about 4 inches (10 cm) below the soil surface. Fill around the plant with soil.

▼ Spanish bluebell (*Hyacinthoides hispanica*) is one of the most faithful spring bulbs. It returns year after year.

▲ Anybody with an interest in agriculture and the past who finds themselves in the vicinity of Hamburg would do well to visit the living history museum Freilichtmuseum am Kiekeberg. It has been a source of inspiration for Michael's building projects and gardening. The museum is renowned for its plant markets, which are held in April and August (see the website for times and dates).

◄ Heidi and Michael collect small milk churns whenever they come across them at flea markets. They have a penchant for old farm collectables and rarities, and the little museum features farmhouse paraphernalia as well as tools. Local people and museum visitors sometimes turn up with new items for the museum, often when clearing out the house of a deceased relative. Rather than throwing out old artifacts, they donate them to the museum instead.

The farm is a prime example of careful restoration—so much so that it has attracted attention in professional circles. The Schleswig-Holstein State Office for the Preservation of Historical Monuments awarded Heidi and Michael a certificate of achievement in 2015. The previous year, they won second prize in a competition for Germany's most beautiful garden.

The original apple trees are quite old. Given that they will one day succumb to the ravages of time, Michael has already planted new ones that will eventually replace them. The varieties have been carefully chosen, some for historical reasons.

▲ The garden features multiple beautiful columbine beds in the most endearing colors and shapes. When they bloom in early June, it's a sign of impending summer. They reproduce very easily, which I find a great advantage but others consider a nuisance. I'd say it's a pretty good problem to have! If the self-seeding does become too much for you, just trim the plants before the seeds mature. That's what I do in my garden. Another benefit is that if you cut the stems far enough down near the ground, it encourages new and fresh foliage. This double-flowering type is called 'Granny's Bonnet'. And when you look at the beautiful flowers, you can see why. Heidi really likes this variant and lets them self-seed to their hearts' content.

◀ A few columbines and foxgloves (*Digitalis*) have self-seeded and formed a perfect partnership. Reaching skywards against the half-timbered wall, they are the very essence of the cottage garden.

▶ The purple cranesbill (*Geranium × magnificum*) is a beautiful, robust wild species. An excellent choice if you're going for the natural look, it comes in numerous varieties.

▼ Lupins are a perfect match for the natural aesthetic of the cottage garden. They grow almost anywhere but thrive in light, barren, rocky, and sandy soil—which is why you often see them on the edge of ditches and in gravel pits. Lupins have a remarkable ability to increase the soil's nitrogen content by binding it from the air. They do so using rhizobium, a nitrogen-fixing bacterium that lives in the root nodules of leguminous plants.

◀ Michael also designed and built a little garden house with a built-in stone oven and tiled roof. Heidi bakes bread here, just as the farmers did in days gone by. She uses firewood to preheat the oven a couple of hours in advance, pushing the embers to the side when they are warm enough. The oven stays warm for an incredibly long time because the thick clay wall absorbs the heat.

▼ Poppies are a standard in the cottage garden, both annuals and perennials. *Papaver orientale*, a large poppy with impressive red flowers, is one of the perennials. One minor disadvantage of perennial poppies is that they die back after flowering. In my garden, I solve this problem by planting summer flowers as soon as that happens. I rarely have any bare soil in my garden.

▲ I sometimes photograph the same gardens several times over the course of a season, which shows just how much changes in a matter of weeks. From the beginning of June, things move really fast. This picture shows how little bare soil is left when the perennials are in full swing. Over the next few months, right up to autumn, there's always something in bloom.

▶ The blue-violet flowers scattered around the garden beds are the beautiful *Hesperis matronalis*, which has many names, including dame's violet and night-scented gilliflower. It is a biennial, which means that it does not bloom until the year after the seeds are sown. An evergreen rosette appears in the first season, and it starts to grow upwards in the next. When in bloom in early June, it emits the most beautiful, violet-like scent, especially in the evening. After flowering, the plant goes to seed and then dies back. The other plant with the green inflorescences is Turkish sage *(Phlomis russeliana)*. The flowers on this sublimely architectural plant are an almost straw-like shade of yellow.

▲ The roses bloom around midsummer. Heidi and Michael's garden is home to over one hundred species and varieties. Many are heirloom types, which fit perfectly in this setting. The rose with the delicate yellow flowers is called 'Harison's Yellow'. It is not all that common, which is a pity because its exquisitely delicate flowers and fine rosehips make it really quite special.

◀ Heidi and Michael spend many hours in the garden every day.

▶ The yellow daylily (*Hemerocallis lilioasphodelus*) is a wild species. As the name suggests, its flowers only last a single day, but new buds appear all the time.

There is a marked contrast between the wild planting and the cultivated kitchen garden seen on the next couple of pages. The trick is getting them to work together and playfully interact, a delicate balancing act Heidi and Michael have mastered. The ox-eye daisy (*Leucanthemum vulgare*) grows naturally in the meadow and was already there when Heidi and Michael moved in. It grows on nutrient-poor pastures, arable land, and meadows.

▶ Bold red has long been frowned upon in more romantic gardens, but the color is most welcome in the cottage garden. Think, for example, of poppies—both large perennials and the young and more fleeting common red variety. Here, it is the water avens (*Geum rivale* 'Mrs. J. Bradshaw').

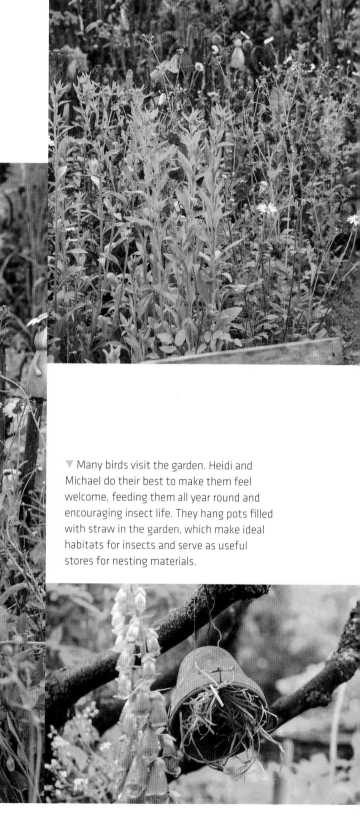

▼ Many birds visit the garden. Heidi and Michael do their best to make them feel welcome, feeding them all year round and encouraging insect life. They hang pots filled with straw in the garden, which make ideal habitats for insects and serve as useful stores for nesting materials.

▲ Its medium-sized, apricot-colored blooms make the climbing rose 'François Juranville' absolutely irresistible. That they also smell great is an added bonus. The clematis, in shades of pink and lavender, is called 'Dr. Ruppel'.

◄ Heidi and Michael tell me they've given up the fight against bishop's weed in several parts of the garden. Now, they just live with it and enjoy the beautiful umbels, here alongside the rose 'Rosa Mundi'.

▶ Wild plants, such as the red campion (*Silene dioica*) self-seed all over the garden.

▶ 'Nanette', an
heirloom rose with
full pink flowers,
is also known as a
Gallica or French rose.
Documented since the
Middle Ages, its genes
are found in many
modern hybrids and
varieties. This group
of flowers is originally
from the Middle
East, the Caucasus,
and southern and
southeastern Europe.
It is easy to care for
and likes warm, well-
drained, preferably
calcareous soil.

▼ Susi, the Persian
cat, likes to follow me
around when I visit,
waiting patiently as
I line up my shots.

△ Around midsummer, the meadow—which was little more than a green carpet during spring (see page 46)—is transformed into a beautiful sea of flowers. The common red poppy (*Papaver rhoeas*), blue cornflower (*Centaurea cyanus*) and corncockle (*Agrostemma githago*) are in full bloom.

◀ Groups of purple cranesbills (*Geranium × magnificum*) also grow in the meadow.

▶ The gas plant, or dittany (*Dictamnus albus*), is a beautiful perennial with a fascinating history. The stems and leaves are covered with bristles and seedpods that secrete flammable oil.

I've always been fascinated by meadows full of flowers but have never grown one. According to Michael, the main thing is that the space—in this case, their meadow—is open to the sun. One winter, he removed the grass and the top layer of soil and sprinkled the patch with a layer of sand. Next, he added turf and straw, burned the top, and pulverized the ash layer. Early the following spring, he sowed a ready-made meadow seed mixture into the sandy and ash-filled soil. Finally, he covered the whole area with a few inches of soil mix. A few months later, the first flowers burst out.

The profusion of flowers is at its most intense around midsummer. The cornflowers, in particular, bloom for quite some time. In late summer or autumn, Michael tills the meadow with a hoe and then rakes everything up to prevent the cuttings from nourishing the soil (see the picture on page 68). It is important to keep the soil relatively barren.

▲ Heidi is particularly keen on the single-flowered peonies because it is easier for bees to access the pollen on the stamens. This gorgeous variety—'Bowl of Beauty'—was already in the garden when Heidi and Michael bought the place. Although surrounded by very tall grass, it bloomed merrily. Since then, the couple has divided it again and again, and it is now sprinkled around the garden.

◀ The white peony 'Krinkled White' is robust and flowers well once it catches on. Peonies may look delicate but are among the hardiest of garden perennials. They prefer a sunny spot, and if the conditions are right, they will flower every year. The stems emerge in early spring and grow rapidly by the day.

▲ The climbing rose 'Veilchenblau' ('Violet Blue') has a distinct bluish hue that catches the eye. It has multiple alternative names: 'Bleu-Violet', 'Blue Rambler', and 'Blue Rosalie'. Here, it is seen growing up a tree. Given that it gladly produces an abundance of buds and flowers every year, it clearly thrives in this spot.

▶ Most heirloom roses bloom only once per season, but 'Rosa de Rescht' blooms twice. It was discovered a little over a hundred years ago in Rasht (Iran), on the trade route between China and Persia, hence the name.

► Heidi fell for this
'Rosarium Uetersen'
rose because it
complements the
wood on the half-
timbered house.

▲ 'Heidi just calls
this one "the peony."
Whatever its official
designation, it is
exquisite.

▼ 'Leander' is a
climbing rose by the
English gardener
David Austin.

▲ When Heidi and Michael took over the house in 1993, the original roof was in very poor condition and leaked badly. But they were never in any doubt that they would rethatch it. Thatch is not so popular these days because of its relatively limited shelf life compared to other materials. On a south-facing side, it is expected to last twenty to forty years at most, on the north, forty to sixty. Fire insurance is also expensive for thatched houses. But it's terrific that some people are willing to ignore such practical considerations and let beauty prevail.

◀ There are so many different bellflowers, both annual summer ones and perennials. What they all have in common is the botanical name *Campanula*. The lavender-blue flower in the picture is a perennial called *Campanula lactiflora*, specifically 'Prichard's Variety' of milky bellflower.

▶▶ 'Chianti' will undoubtedly make many readers think of red wine. It is an apt name for this deep-red rose by the English breeder David Austin.

◀ From time to time, the couple give objects from the museum an airing.

▶ Tread carefully! Chickens of all sizes roam free in the garden. But don't worry, they're very tame.

▲ 'Raubritter' is a stunning rose with almost spherical flowers, reminiscent of those painted by the artist J. L. Jensen (1800–1856). This might lead you to think that 'Raubritter' is an heirloom rose, but it wasn't introduced until 1936. In 1966, the Old Garden Rose Committee of the American Rose Society defined an heirloom rose as pre-1867, the year the first hybrid tea rose, 'La France', saw the light of day. Tea hybrid roses are what we now call modern roses.

◀ The garden valerian (*Valeriana officinalis*) is a beautiful plant about 6.5 feet (2 m) tall with pale pink umbels and a delightful scent. It is absolutely perfect for adding height and generating a slightly wild look.

▲ The white climbing Rosa 'Alba Maxima' has long, graceful shoots.
Its origin is unknown, but European sources mention it as far back
as 1400. Like most heirloom roses, it blooms only once
a season but produces the most beautiful rosehips in August.
Like all Alba roses, it has a sublime scent—one that connoisseurs
claim is unmatched. It is also a very robust rose that looks great
in shrubbery. Rosa 'Alba Maxima' features in the famous artist P.
S. Krøyer's (1851–1909) painting *Garden Party with Marie Krøyer and
Roses* (1893).

▶ Heidi and Michael's garden is teeming with wildlife. The meadow
attracts a lot of insects that add to the life cycle of the habitat they
have created. Ladybugs are famously fond of aphids, but ticks,
beetles, hoverflies, and parasitic wasps also consume harmful
insects. This little insect hotel has many nooks and crannies in
which important species ensconce themselves.

▲ As mentioned earlier, it is important that the meadow is mowed and plowed once the flowers have shed their seeds. If the cuttings are left lying about, they will nourish the soil, which means next season's grass will grow too fast and suffocate the flowers. Over the summer, Heidi and Michael regularly remove unwanted mugwort, nettles, and thistles, among others, to prevent them from multiplying.

▶ Few flowers are as closely associated with the cottage garden and farmhouse idyll as the hollyhock. You often see them planted up against a house wall, but they also make a delightful addition to garden beds.

A tip: To stop hollyhocks from tipping over, cut off the stems about 4 inches (10 cm) above the ground once they reach a height of about 3.3 feet (1 m). That way new stems grow but only to about 5 feet (1.5 m), and they won't need support.

▶▶ The tree mallow (*Lavatera rosea*) is related to the hollyhock. The family resemblance is unmistakable.

◀ *Clematis viticella* 'Dark Eyes' is one of the darkest varieties of clematis. It is late-flowering and had just appeared when this photograph was taken in July. If you cut *Clematis viticella* all the way down in the fall or winter, it will bloom again, as do all late-flowering clematis.

▶ Sweet William (*Dianthus barbatus*) is propagated from seeds and looks good in beds and bouquets.

▲ My last visit to the garden was a wonderful late-summer day toward the end of August. Goldenrod (*Solidago*) was in bloom here and there in natural clusters in the grass, which had been trimmed around the plants. In a standard herbaceous border, think twice before planting goldenrod, as it propagates by throwing out suckers.

◀ *Polygonum orientale* goes by the wonderful name kiss-me-over-the-garden-gate.

▶ You should also sow sweet pea (*Lathyrus odoratus*) from seed every year.

▲ The garden phlox (*Phlox paniculata*) is a charming perennial, to which I will return later in the book. It blooms in July and August and really lights up the garden with its beautiful flowers, which also have the loveliest scent. There are many varieties—this one is 'Younique Old Pink'. Divide phlox every three or four years. In the fall, dig up the root ball and pull the stems apart.

▶ The Japanese anemone 'Queen Charlotte' (*Anemone japonica*), is an old classic that seems very much at home here. In fact, it thrives in all sorts of gardens—some consider it almost a weed because it can be a little too eager and spread wildly. For some unknown reason, I have never had any success with this lovely late-summer plant. I have tried many times, but it resolutely refuses to grow in my garden. It is fascinating how plants that thrive in one setting just won't grow in another.

◀ A self-seeded hollyhock. It is always exciting waiting to see what color will emerge from a seed-producing plant, as they often vary somewhat from the mother plant. If you want to propagate and be sure of the color, divide or take cuttings.

Really Wild

The first Danish garden I want to introduce is in the north of the island of Zealand and belongs to Susanne Jacobi and Børge Riget Nielsen. They have spent over thirty years creating a beautifully relaxed space in a very pure cottage garden style, complete with a lush kitchen garden, crooked old trees, homemade garden furniture, chickens, ducks, and an abundance of wildflowers—many self-seeded—that attract a wealth of insects. All that's missing is a thatched roof and half-timbered farmhouse! But as it happens, the couple's home is very cozy and full of soul—a beautiful yellow-brick edifice with a charming wooden extension in blue. It is evident that creative people live here.

A bit of a sad sight greeted the couple the first time they saw the place. The house had been empty for some time. Around it lay a large, sloping plot full of long grass and three old cherry trees. But Susanne and Børge saw its potential, and over the years, the garden has sprouted new features as their requirements have changed and their four children left the nest. When they no longer needed a big lawn for the kids to play on, they extended the kitchen garden.

The 20- to 23-foot (6- to 7-m) slope was a challenge, but Susanne and Børge were unfazed. Over the years, they have carved out plots and terraces and laid stairs and paths. "It was quite a bit of work," they say, wildly understating it! Both helped lay the stones, which they sourced from nearby fields.

Much may have changed over the decades, but there was never a grand plan. Indeed, they often change their minds to make parts of the garden less labor-intensive. A garden like this is hard work, but these days they also need time for travel and for their eight grandchildren. The garden must not become a chore—it's okay to rein in ambitions.

Susanne and Børge work on the garden together and have a shared passion for all things gardening in general. They often visit other gardens on vacation, including in England, visits that inspired the design of their own at home and its selection of plants and flowers.

They grow most of the flowers from their own seeds and cuttings, but from time to time, they pick up a few plants on their travels.

Most of the plants in the garden are old acquaintances. The main point is that they should be easy to grow, reliable, preferably attract insects and birds, and maybe make a nice bouquet or two. It's all so lovely.

You can't help but marvel at the lushness of it all. Many gardeners dream of this kind of place—especially younger ones who don't want everything to look overly managed and scripted. It may look easy, but this is great (garden) art.

Follow Susanne and her garden on Instagram: @sus_jacobi.

▲ It's early May. The kitchen garden is freshly planted, and a new season beckons. The edible produce is mostly Børge's doing. He grew up with a big herb garden and really enjoys growing his own food. The kitchen garden takes up a lot of the approximately 1,700-square-yard (1,400 sq m) site. In summer, this part of the garden is home to more than just herbs. Self-seeded plants pop up. He leaves them alone as long as they don't get in the way or cast shadows over the crops.

◄ Susanne and Børge made the beautiful chairs, which are shown in more detail on the previous page, from willow and hazel. They are always popular with summer visitors.

▲ The soil here is very sandy, so every year, Børge enriches it with homemade compost, chicken droppings from their own animals, and horse manure that they buy. Susanne and Børge are pretty good with their hands and prefer the things they make to have a homemade look. The backbone of any cottage garden is its own distinctive personality. The long, narrow pieces of willow on top of the iron arches are used to support pumpkins. To the right, wire fences stand ready to support climbing peas.

▶ Rows of delicious herbs. This is garlic, which can be harvested up to midsummer. The cloves are planted in the fall.

▼ Siberian bugloss (*Brunnera macrophylla*) is a sweet spring growth that blossoms in May and looks fantastic alongside the spring bulbs.

◀ I'm pretty sure a lot of people mistake Siberian bugloss for ordinary forget-me-nots, but this is a perennial. Forget-me-nots bloom only once then fade away. There are various types. This one, with the beautiful, variegated leaves, is 'Jack Frost'. A similar variety, with identical leaves and white flowers, is called 'Mr. Morse'.

▲ In some gardens (like Heidi and Michael Chalupka's in the previous section), hens roam freely. Not here. They would wreak havoc in the kitchen garden, unable to resist a dust bath in the sandy soil. The couple keep several breeds, including an old English Light Sussex, which Børge says is a perfect "beginner hen." Its calm temperament makes it suitable for families with children. The Light Sussex lays plenty of eggs—even in winter—is a good brood hen and thrives alongside other garden breeds. It is also beautiful, with light feathers and dark markings on the neck, wings, and tail.

▶ 'Purissima' is a faithful white tulip that returns year after year. The problem with some tulips is that they bloom for just a single season and disappear. Not this one.

◀ Silver dollar (*Lunaria annua*) is a real cottage garden plant with beautiful purple flowers and decorative seedheads that resemble coins.

▲ To really come into their own, alliums like *Allium aflatunense* need to be planted in big groups. They bloom in early June, and the green seedheads still look decorative once the flowers have died back.

◀ The purple cranesbill (*Geranium × magnificum*), with its blue-violet flowers, is a classic.

▶ Bigroot geranium (*Geranium macrorrhizum*) 'Czakor' forms a dense carpet and stays green all year round.

▼ Red valerian (*Centranthus ruber*), also known as Jupiter's beard, is a resilient and undemanding perennial that loves a sandy, rocky, and well-drained bed, so it is often seen by the coast. In northern Zealand, it grows pretty much everywhere, between tiles and cobblestones, on roadsides and stone walls. There is also a white-flowering variety, *Centranthus ruber* 'Albus'.

▲ Susanne and Børge have propagated many of the garden's flowers from seed, and there are usually some left over. Susanne sells them at a very reasonable price from a roadside honor system stand. People often stop to check what's on offer. Today it is columbine, but the selection changes during the season.

THE MONEY IS PLACED IN THE MAILBOX, PLEASE.

▲ 'Louise Odier', one of the most famous heirloom roses, launched in France in 1851. The beautifully round pink flowers have numerous petals reminiscent of a tutu. It also has a highly delicate scent. It is one of the Bourbon roses—a group that includes many beautiful varieties, including 'Mme. Isaac Pereire', 'Reine Victoria' and 'Souvenir de la Malmaison'.

▼ Few flowers are as closely associated with the cottage garden as poppies, and some of the most impressive are the so-called opium poppies (*Papaver somniferum*). They may look delicate, but don't be fooled—propagating them from seed is pretty straightforward. If you only have them in the garden once and let the seeds sprinkle on bare soil, you can be absolutely sure they'll be back again the following year. Once the petals have fallen off, you are left with beautiful gray-green seedheads.

◀ Sweet William is such a sweet name for a sweet plant. *Dianthus barbatus* is often thought of as a summer plant—an annual—but when the winters are particularly mild, it behaves like a perennial and returns year after year, especially if it is trimmed back to the ground in the fall.

▲ A fence bounds the lower part of the garden to keep the ducks (see next page) away from the flower beds. The fence accentuates the cottage atmosphere, as do the foxgloves spread around the property. Their upright stems add variation to the perennial bed and are a beautiful accompaniment to the roses, which are at their tallest around midsummer (as seen here). The large boxwood tree was originally a very small shrub. Børge has been pruning it for almost three decades.

▶ The peach-leaved bellflower (*Campanula persicifolia*) is another good self-seeder. Unlike the poppies on the previous page, it is a perennial. It is ideal for beds but also works very well in bouquets, for example, with roses.This fine bellflower is available in several shades of blue, as well as white and pink.

▲ Susanne and Børge keep Muscovy ducks for several reasons. The most important one is that the ducks love slugs. Unfortunately, they are equally keen on many of the crops in the kitchen garden, especially lettuce and seedlings, so they have to be confined to the lower part of the garden.

Hi Dorthe!

Remember to close the gate behind you when you go in to collect eggs. The chickens are inquisitive and will escape into the garden if they can.

Thanks, Børge

◀ It's important to have good friends and acquaintances to look after the animals and water the plants when you're away, and it's nice to be able to return the favor at some point.

▶ 'Black Peony' (*Papaver somniferum*), a rich, deep-black opium poppy, is the most beautiful of the peony poppies—at least I think so. This one grows true from seed, and the seedlings are identical to their mother plant.

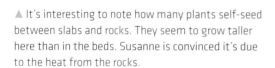

▲ It's interesting to note how many plants self-seed between slabs and rocks. They seem to grow taller here than in the beds. Susanne is convinced it's due to the heat from the rocks.

▶ This beautiful delphinium has self-seeded, so the couple does not know its name. It looks nothing like any of the other delphiniums in the garden. Like many other plants when they crossbreed, you're never sure what will emerge. Plants that self-seed in the soil are often more robust than those we plant. Susanne and Børge have spent several summers eagerly anticipating this special delphinium.

◀ Susanne and Børge keep several chicken breeds in the run, including the Easter egger, which comes in white, black, brown, or gray. The name stems from the beautiful light-green eggs they lay. The couple also keep beautiful Black Forest hens, which are very calm and trusting.

◀ When it comes
to self-seeding, the
Macedonian scabious
or pincushion flower
(*Knautia macedonica*)
is a real winner. In
early spring, countless
plants pop up among
the pebbles on the
path. It's an easy
and undemanding
perennial.

▼ The snapdragon
(*Antirrhinum majus*)
grows well in pots
and is good for
bouquet cutting.

▲ Compare these pictures with those on pages 74–75, and you'll see just how much has happened in the kitchen garden in a few months. Everything seems like it's growing with great abandon, but great care has also been taken. The garden is intensively cultivated in a sustainable way. As soon as one crop is finished, a new one takes over.

◀ The geraniums enjoy outdoor life until late summer, when they are moved into a bright cellar. They continue to bloom there but become more lanky as they seek the light. In the spring, Susanne and Børge cut back and repot the geraniums.

▲ The milky bellflower (*Campanula lactiflora*) 'Prichard's Variety' is a popular perennial—understandably so, as its lavender-blue flowers are compatible with just about every type of garden.

The drawback with bellflowers is that they almost always fall over at about 6 feet (2 m) tall. There are two solutions: either support the stems before the problem arises or get the pruning shears out around June. At that point, the stems are around 3 feet (1 m) high, and you should cut them down to around half of that height. This produces offshoots a bit shorter than the original main ones would have been. The shrub then grows to only about 5 feet (1.5 m) and stands up on its own. You also get a lot more—but smaller—flowers. You also delay the flowering by a few weeks until early August.

◄ The red lupin (*Lupinus polyphyllus*) 'Gallery Red' has remarkable hues found nowhere else in the wild.

▼ Small groups of arranged pots create a welcoming, fun ambience. Note the willow branches Susanne has woven around the outside of the rainwater barrel. She has worked with willow for years and runs basket-weaving courses. She also used to grow various varieties of willow.

▲ A small geranium in a clay pot is a lovely, inexpensive gift. It is pretty easy to get geraniums to take root in spring. First, remove the lower leaves from the top shoots and any buds. This will stop the cutting from expending energy on flowers instead of roots. Next, plant the shoot in moist soil, in a warm spot but not in direct sunlight. It will take root after about three weeks.

▼ 'Heidelberg', a beautiful climbing rose with a rich, enticing color, snakes its way up the house.

▼ 'Summerwind' is a romantic rose with ruffled blooms and a lovely, subtle scent. The pink flowers are particularly striking against the dark shed.

◄ This rosebush is a magnificent specimen. From a purely photographic perspective, I could hardly have chosen a better day to see it. Taking photographs of roses is all a matter of timing. Arrive too early—before they are properly in bloom—and you are likely to be disappointed. But don't wait too long either, as there is nothing as sad as a rose as it starts to fade away.

▲ One of the most beautiful roses I have ever seen—and which I also have in my garden—is 'Alchymist'. This is a climbing rose with exquisite flowers and an irresistible scent. The color varies somewhat, occasionally verging on pink, but usually is described as apricot-colored.

'Alchymist' was introduced in 1956 by the German breeder Kordes. Since 1887, Kordes has brought hundreds of beautiful roses to market. 'Alchymist' is one of its most popular and well-loved varieties. However, there is a slight hitch. Unfortunately, 'Alchymist' only blooms once per season. All the more reason to enjoy it when it does, I say!

▼ 'Ghislaine de Féligonde' is another apricot-colored rose with numerous but modestly sized ruffled petals. Some roses are difficult to identify, but this one is unmistakable. Its plentiful buds and small, dense bouquets of flowers make it highly distinctive. The individual flowers vary from apricot to ochre yellow and white, depending on the stage they are at in the cycle.

▲ If I were asked to rank the top flowers for the cottage garden, the common foxglove (*Digitalis purpurea*), which pops up regularly in this book, would be very high on the list. It's lovely and so easy to grow. Just sprinkle seeds on a bare piece of land. They germinate in early spring, and the large rosettes they form during the summer stay green throughout winter. The following year, around midsummer, the beautiful foxgloves open up, and then the plant withers and dies. The variety shown here is called 'Sutton's Apricot'.

▲ *Cosmos bipinnatus*, commonly known as garden cosmos or Mexican aster, is one of the easiest summer flowers. Sow in early May, and they will bloom ten to twelve weeks later. A fantastic bouquet flower, as well as an excellent bed filler between perennials, it comes in many colors and heights. This hybrid is called 'Sensation Mix'.

▶ Another foxglove (*Digitalis purpurea*). The variety is called 'Pam's Choice'. There are both monochromatic and spotted varieties, all of which are beautiful in their own way.

▲ Dill is not only a wonderful culinary ingredient, but also its yellow-green umbels make a lovely addition to bouquets.

◄ Susanne likes to grow flowers for bouquets. The sweet pea (*Lathyrus odoratus*) is a must, especially if you like fragrant flowers—and most people do!

▼ Ducks need access to water to keep their plumage healthy.

A Clear Favorite

It's time now to visit one of my absolute favorites—Wollerton Old Hall in Shropshire, England. One thing I find fascinating about this place is the unique layout. It combines large and small spaces, captivating plantings, stunning vistas, and beautiful details, making it one of England's most remarkable private gardens.

In total, it covers about nine acres (four hectares) and has so much going on in it, including a water garden, a green garden, a perennial garden, and one garden solely in warm tones. And then there is the Rose and Sundial Garden (shown here), with its distinctive and charming cottage atmosphere.

Lesley and John Jenkins bought Wollerton Old Hall in 1983. The house, the history of which goes all the way back to the Middle Ages, needed some tender loving care—to put it mildly. But what about the garden? According to Lesley, it was just a big, empty plot covered in wild vegetation, self-seeded trees, and old junk. The couple rolled up their sleeves and got to work.

The main reason for buying the property was to create a garden in the style of Sissinghurst Castle and Hidcote Manor, albeit on a smaller scale, and their efforts have truly borne fruit. The garden architect is Lesley, a former art historian who threw herself into the project. The first step was to design the hedges, trees, paths, pavements, buildings, seating, and lawns. Then the major construction work began. It was quite a task.

The site is smaller than the two iconic gardens mentioned prior but still around 48,000 square yards (40,000 sq m)—equivalent to four soccer fields. Admittedly, not all of that space is taken up by garden, but it is still on a scale that most people would find daunting. However, Lesley had the support of John, a physicist with a keen interest in plants. The two embarked on the project together.

The fact that it is a private garden means it oozes personality. Most gardens of this size in England are run by the National Trust, an organization that has been preserving old buildings and gardens for over a century, usually after the owners have passed away, as was the case for Sissinghurst Castle Garden and Hidcote Manor Garden. In fact, Hidcote was the first garden to be taken over by the Trust back in 1948.

As the old saying goes, "The garden is the gardener," which suggests that when the creator of a garden passes away, the spirit of the garden is lost as well.

A garden is a living organism—it must never become static and stagnant. The National Trust does great work, but its focus is on preservation, not progress.

Lesley recalls how she and John have adapted and perfected their design and approach to the plants over the years. I have done much the same in my garden, establishing new spaces, cutting down hedges, adding buildings, and constantly rethinking and changing plants.

Wollerton Old Hall is one of the most frequently visited private gardens in England. Guests arrive by the car- and busload from early spring to late summer. Many of them are tourists from overseas who are in England just to visit its lush gardens.

The garden is open several days a week throughout the season. Read more at www.wollertonoldhallgarden.com and follow it on Instagram: @wollertonohg.

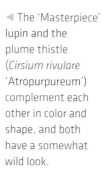

▲ Wollerton Old Hall is a proper Arts and Crafts garden. Arts and Crafts was a late nineteenth-century movement in Britain, a reaction to the industrial revolution and mass production. One of its founders was the English artist, socialist, and author William Morris (1834–1896).

◄ The 'Masterpiece' lupin and the plume thistle (*Cirsium rivulare* 'Atropurpureum') complement each other in color and shape, and both have a somewhat wild look.

▶ German bearded iris (*Iris germanica*) is a sun worshipper. Make sure its thick roots (rhizomes) are free of soil. Plant it right on the surface. There are many hundreds, maybe thousands, of different varieties. This lavender-colored one is called 'Susan Bliss'.

▲ A large group of German bearded iris (*Iris germanica*). This lavender-colored variety is called 'Jane Phillips'. Given a sunny, drained place to grow, the bearded iris is a very hardy perennial, especially if you occasionally dig up the root stalks—the rhizomes—divide them, and replant the smaller pieces.

▶ Siberian iris (*Iris sibirica*) is delicate and graceful. It is available in several varieties, although not as many as the German bearded iris. This one is called 'Sparkling Rose'. Like all other irises, it likes the sun but is a little more tolerant of and will even bloom in partial shade.

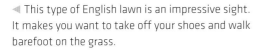

◀ This type of English lawn is an impressive sight. It makes you want to take off your shoes and walk barefoot on the grass.

▲ If there is one thing the English are good at, it is planting roses and perennials together to form a symbiotic whole. No bare stalks or exposed soil here! The faintly yellow rose is 'Crocus Rose', also bred by David Austin. It is such a delicate bloom that it works well with pretty much everything, including the pretty little blood-red cranesbill (*Geranium sanguineum* var. *striatum*).

◀ Cranesbills come in an incredible range of varieties, and most of them go well with roses. One example is the wood cranesbill (*Geranium sylvaticum*) 'Mayflower' with its beautiful lavender-blue flowers, which thrive in both sun and partial shade.

► Golden Celebration' is another of the yellow Austin roses, perhaps the best and most beautiful of them all—at least according to David Austin (1926–2018). Austin was a pioneer rose breeder who will go down in history as the creator of the English roses—a group notable for their nostalgic charm and unsurpassed scent.

He lived near Wollerton Old Hall and was a close friend of Lesley and John. He often visited them and named a rose after their garden in 2011. Although exquisite, it is quite hard to grow and thus not very common, which is a shame.

▼ Macedonian scabious, *Knautia macedonica*, seen here growing freely, adds a hint of "wildness."

▼ The scarlet leather flower (*Clematis texensis*) 'Etoile Rose' is a highly distinctive clematis with the tulip-shaped flowers characteristic of the *texensis* species. All the varieties in this species are late-flowering, which means you need to trim them back to the ground by early spring to make sure they grow fresh shoots capable of flowering.

▲ 'Olivia Rose Austin' is named after David Austin's granddaughter. Austin will always be remembered as one of the greats for his ability to crossbreed old heirloom roses with modern hybrid tea roses. In doing so, he combined the best of both worlds—the beautiful shape and amazing fragrance of the heirloom roses and the modern hybrid tea roses' ability to rebloom.

◄ ► Honeysuckle (*Lonicera*) is a classic cottage garden plant. It smells great (hence the name) and is undeniably beautiful, especially alongside roses in a bouquet. It doesn't get much more romantic than that.

▲ Yet another cranesbill that lights up the bed with its pink flowers. This is a purely wild species, the Armenian cranesbill (*Geranium psilostemon*). It is notable for its pink flowers arranged around a striking black center. This type of cranesbill requires support—in this case, from the surrounding plants. You can also use pruned branches in early spring.

▶ The rose 'Rhapsody in Blue' and clematis 'Warszawska Nike', the colors of which are more or less identical, make a perfect match. 'Warszawska Nike' is another clematis that you need to cut back all the way down to the soil before spring, because new blooms only emerge from new growth. Quite a few other clematis varieties don't need to be pruned because they bloom on the previous year's growth.

◀ The Arts and Crafts movement used organic, curving forms inspired by nature. It also championed the use of local materials. Its influence is visible here, for example, in the consistent use of oak for doors, fences, and pergolas and the simplicity of the design.

▲ Note the precise lines at the edge of the lawn. This is high-quality work. The head gardener, Phil, has the help of one other gardener and several volunteers, who work hard to maintain the garden.

◀ Dahlias are used as bed-fillers to cover any bare patches of soil. This apricot-colored variety is known, appropriately enough, as 'Apricot Desire'.

▶ Pearl of Heemstede' is a well-known and classic dahlia with rose-hued and pink flowers.

▲ 'Rosa Pastell' (Phlox paniculata) is just one of many beautiful phlox varieties.

▶ 'Rhapsody in Blue' is one of the most recognizable roses, with a striking color that many—myself included—find extremely beautiful.

◀ When garden phlox (*Phlox paniculata*) thrives, it self-seeds, and new color variants emerge, such as the one pictured here. There's no denying how gorgeous it is.

▶ 'Wildeve' is another Austin rose, seen here in captivating company with horn violet (*Viola cornuta*). This is a purely wild species, which differs slightly from the bred ones widely available in garden centers in springtime. What's special about the wild version is that it is a perennial, although it does not flower for very long.

◀ The beautiful old barn adds to the cottage feel. It looks like it's always been there, but it was designed by Lesley. The timber was carefully selected at a sawmill. But the roof is old, procured from a company specializing in vintage building materials. There are a number of such companies in England.

▶ Immaculate hedges delineate the varied spaces in the garden. Phil and his team are very dedicated to their work. The garden is full of brilliantly executed details—especially the fantastic layout and long vistas.

◀ Garden phlox thrives here and plays a very important role in the overall effect. This variety is known as 'Bright Eyes'.

▼ 'Tenor', with its pink flowers, is a beautiful garden phlox. Note how it stands out against the green background. Fitting it in is sometimes a challenge, but the balance is just right in this spot.

A Clear Favorite   103

Just Like in England

Judging by the picture, you'd probably think this house is somewhere in England—but it's not! This unique house and garden may exhibit the traditional English cottage style, but they are located in the south of the island of Zealand, Denmark.

Sanne Damore and her husband, Carsten Schjødt, fell head over heels for this place—a former psychiatric hospital—and snapped it up in 2010. The garden was massively overgrown, but they rolled up their sleeves and tore into it.

There is a good reason why this place looks English. It's a faithful copy of a gardener's home Ida Marie Suhr (1853–1938) saw in England. It was so unusually beautiful and harmonious that she built an exact copy when she decided to open a psychiatric institution. Building work was completed in 1892. The institution housed rooms where a nurse treated poor people from the local community, and it also played host to a Sunday school.

Suhr was one of the wealthiest Danish women of her day. She was deeply modest but extremely generous when it came to the estate staff and the poor and vulnerable of the parish. In addition to Langebæk Asylum, she built a number of high-quality, aesthetically beautiful homes for her employees.

As mentioned, Sanne and Carsten jumped at the chance to take it over—even though the garden and house both needed a lot of TLC. The couple is not afraid of hard work, and Carsten is very good with his hands.

While they were refurbishing the interior, Sanne began to think about the garden. A Danish gardening show, *Haven i Hune* (*The Garden in Hune*), had kindled her interest in gardening. She says it was "like going to gardening school." Later, she also discovered the joys of BBC *Gardeners' World* (see pages 30–31). What better time to watch English gardening TV than when you've just bought an English-style house? Sanne and Carsten derived plenty of ideas from the show and soon turned their attention to planning the garden.

Haven i Hune was hosted by Anne Just and featured the landscape architect Kjeld Slot. Sanne admired his approach and invited him to Langebæk in 2014. A host of ideas emerged from that meeting. The couple envisioned a garden with multiple small areas separated by beech hedges. Kjeld suggested following the lines of the half-timbering on the building. It was a highly adaptable concept and just the kind of inspiration the couple wanted. Before long, Sanne and Carsten had cleared most of the ground but left some trees and shrubs standing. Next, they started sinking posts and stretching out string to mark the layout.

As the snow fell in winter 2015, Sanne paced the length of the strings, her footprints making it easier to see the lines from the first-floor window.

Just Like in England   105

▲ In February 2015, as soon as the snow melted, Sanne bought four hundred bare-root beech plants to delineate the six spaces in her new garden. The photograph gives you a sense of the layout, even though the plants aren't very tall yet. It will be years before they reach full height, but the old trees add gravitas and help generate the special cottage garden atmosphere.

◀ Another perennial that likes the conditions here is Siberian bugloss (*Brunnera macrophylla*).

▶ Few plants from the original garden remain, but a couple of large groups of peonies have been divided and replanted in an arch-shaped bed.

▼ Behind the house is a space with raised beds where Sanne grows herbs and flowers. Both in terms of size and location, the raised beds echo the lines of the half-timbering. To the right of the house is a fence with gaps in it—the fact that the fence isn't completely solid endows the area with a certain lightness.

▲ Every spring, Sanne has a lot of tulips in pots. When they die back, she removes the whole clump and lays it out to dry. She doesn't touch the tulips until the tops have faded all the way down. Only then does she separate the bulbs and remove the withered stems. The bulbs are then left to dry in the sun before being planted in the beds in late summer. Once the tulips have been removed from the pots, Sanne plants dahlia bulbs in them.

▲ Feverfew (*Tanacetum parthenium*) is a 16- to 20-inch (40- to 50-cm)-tall annual with a host of small, daisy-like flowers. It is grown from seed and resembles chamomile, only with more beautiful foliage. Feverfew is said to be good for headaches and migraines. A few leaves are enough—but be warned, they don't taste nice! Another good thing about feverfew is that it self-seeds. Once it's established in the garden, it will keep popping up all over the place. Feverfew looks good in garden beds and bouquets. Small flowers are always a wonderful complement to more dominant ones, like roses.

◄ As mentioned, the peonies were already in the garden when Sanne and Carsten moved here, so they are not sure of the name of the species. I think it's *Paeonia lactiflora*, 'Karl Rosenfield' (Chinese or garden peony). This is an older variety found in many old farm gardens in Denmark.

▲ ◄ Peonies blossom in June. The photo shows them side by side with the absolutely indispensable garden lady's mantle (*Alchemilla mollis*), a perennial with many outstanding properties. It is easy to grow, and it has the most beautiful foliage and adorable lime-yellow flowers, which look good in all sorts of contexts and is particularly stunning in bouquets.

▲ Mowing the grass is Carsten's job. In some places, he lets it grow wild and tall because he and Sanne like the natural look. In early spring, daffodils grow on the lawn around the tree, so Carsten doesn't mow there. The foliage needs to fade naturally and in situ to rejuvenate the bulbs.

▶ Goatsbeard (*Aruncus dioicus*) isn't really a shrub. It is a perennial that dies back every fall and reappears in the spring. Fully grown, it is 6 feet (2 m) tall and takes up quite a lot of space. Although not very common these days, it used to be a fixture in many rural gardens, so it fits in perfectly here.

◀ 'Heimdal' Korean lilac (*Syringa meyeri*), a dwarf lilac, blooms in May/June, producing the finest small, fragrant flowers. The shrub rarely grows more than 5 feet (1.5 m) tall.

Just Like in England   109

▲ Carsten prunes the beautiful Cornelian cherry (*Cornus mas*). When they started clearing the grounds, he and Sanne just knew they had to keep the tree. They removed some of the branches, leaving an umbrella-style canopy that provides welcome shade on hot summer days. Sanne adds that the tree is especially beautiful in February/March when it blooms lime-yellow. Bees love it too!

▶▶▶ Perennial sage 'Caradonna', the lupin 'Gallery Red', and columbine are all good, reliable perennials.

▲ As prolific pollinators, bees are one of our most important insects. They buzz around the garden, collecting nectar and pollen, from spring onward. Unfortunately, their numbers are in decline, which has serious consequences for plant life. So, it's a good idea to plant pollen-rich plants like the perennial Oriental poppy (Papaver orientale).

▼ The beautiful climbing rose 'Wild Rover' is purple with a yellow center.

◄ When I ask Sanne to name her favorite among the many roses in the garden, she responds instantly 'Crown Princess Margareta'—because of its lovely fragrance and amber-yellow flower. The rose is named after Crown Princess Margareta of Sweden (1882–1920), granddaughter of Queen Victoria of the United Kingdom (1819–1901) and mother of Queen Margrethe II of Sweden (1910–2000).

▲ It is always good to plant tall. Carsten has built some amazing obelisks (see the picture on page 111), on which Sanne grows clematis. This one, with the beautiful deep purple flowers, is 'Warszawska Nike'.

▶ The orange ball tree (*Buddleja globosa*) is not that common, which is a shame because its orange, spherical inflorescences are strikingly beautiful and irresistible to bees.

◀ Blue lupins and columbines make great neighbors. The two plants go really well together. The lupins, which are often found growing along hedges and ditches, infuse the garden with a touch of the wild.

▲ No, it isn't a weed! This is a beautiful perennial thistle that perfectly matches the color scheme. This is the plume thistle (*Cirsium rivulare*) 'Atropurpureum'. It's a sterile plant, so it doesn't seed the way ordinary thistles do. The only way to multiply it is by dividing.

◄ 'Rose de Rescht', as described on page 62, is a favorite in many gardens.

► *Lychnis coronaria*, rose campion, is notable for its in-your-face shade of pink, but in the right company, its gray stems and foliage are gorgeous.

▲ Some roses, like 'Rose de Rescht' at the bottom of the previous page, are incredibly distinctive and instantly recognizable. But some, especially double roses, are difficult to distinguish from each other. Sanne doesn't know the name of this one, but my good friend and rose expert Ernst Jensen, who frequently helps me out when I'm stuck, is pretty sure it's 'Gertrude Jekyll'. Ernst wrote a highly regarded book, *Et liv med roser* (*A Life with Roses*), the cultivation sections of which are invaluable.

▲ 'Gertrude Jekyll' has beautiful flowers and forms harmonious shrubs. Little wonder English gardeners have twice voted it their favorite rose. It also smells great!

◀ It was the driest summer in memory when I took this picture in 2018. At the time, many plants were struggling from the heat and lack of rain, but not the lamb's ear (*Stachys byzantina*).

Just Like in England   115

▲ ◀ Carsten is really good with his hands. Everything he designs and makes is very precise—like this beautifully proportioned pavilion. Sanne had long wanted a gazebo in a nostalgic style. When Carsten acquired old windows from a local school, he set about making one. The original idea was to plant tomatoes in the structure, but it ended up being a place people hang out in. It's big enough for four people to sit around a table, and there is a lovely view of the yard, the newest of the outdoor spaces. The tiny house is warm and sheltered, so the plan is to grow plants around it that like a bit of warmth (e.g., citrus fruits and olives).

► Carsten took on quite a task when Sanne persuaded him to build twelve raised beds. Again, the half-timbering on the house determined their size and location. After filling them with soil, Sanne planted herbs, vegetables, and flowers, working on the principle of "organized chaos."

▼ The results were somewhat mixed. For example, the cabbages were a real challenge in the first year. It was back to the drawing board for Carsten. He then designed and made racks with black tulle netting that fits snugly on top of the boxes. The net stopped the cabbage butterflies from laying eggs.

▲ In late summer, dahlias brighten up the pots between the raised beds. The orange pompon dahlia 'Bantling' goes well with red brick. Sanne always has dahlias around because they are perfect for bouquets—not to mention in beds. In the fall, she digs up the bulbs and stores them in a frost-free place.

◄ There is nothing quite like a bouquet plucked from the garden. Sanne and Carsten always have flowers on the table.

▶ Every year, Sanne sows summer flowers in the garden and raised beds. Some survive the winter, like the snapdragon (*Antirrhinum majus*). There are so many beautiful varieties—this is 'Black Prince'. It also looks great in bouquets.

▼ Sanne takes great care of the raised beds. She makes her own fertilizer. She fills a giant bricklayer's bucket in the farthest corner of the garden to the brim with stinging nettles and water. This "soup" simmers for two weeks. It smells pretty foul, so she keeps it as far away from the house as possible. She then strains out the nettles and throws them away. Once a week after that, she dilutes the remaining liquid and uses it as fertilizer: 1 part nettle "soup" to 10 parts water. Sanne waters the plants with this mixture in the evening, so the smell evaporates during the night. The next morning, it's obvious the plants have enjoyed a pick-me-up—they are bursting with strength and vitality.

▲ Carsten was a bit surprised to find out just how much you can grow in boxes. He enjoys puttering about with the plants and is convinced a standard garden would have been much more of a hassle. Here, the plants are at eye level, and it doesn't take long to weed a box.

▼ Oskar—one of Sanne and Carsten's four cats—enjoys a nap on the back step.

A New England Garden

I had dreamt of visiting New England for years. The planet really feels smaller these days, especially since I joined Instagram and started following gardeners all over the world.

Suddenly, I could contact people I had previously only read about in books, in articles, and on the internet, or had perhaps seen on TV. I have admired and followed Bunny Williams, the author of several books on interior design, for years now. Her approach to gardening has always fascinated me. For Bunny, a garden is about creating a harmonious whole that also includes the buildings—both exterior and interior. She sees the garden as an extension of the home.

Before we visit Bunny and her garden, I will describe my trip to the United States in brief. In early September 2017, I flew to Boston to embark on a three-week adventure. I had been to New York once, but that was before my interest in gardening really took off. So, you might say this was something of a maiden voyage for me. I was already thinking about this book, so I wanted to visit the small island of Nantucket, about 30 miles (50 km) south of Cape Cod, Massachusetts. I had seen pictures of it online, full of the most charming wooden houses, with picturesque gardens framed by beautiful fences. Roses bloomed in cascades, and bulging plant boxes hung from window ledges. It was an engaging form of abundance. Google "Nantucket" to see what I mean. I found a book called *Nantucket Cottages and Gardens: Charming Spaces on the Faraway Isle* by Leslie Linsley, which was an absolute cornucopia of inspiration. I simply had to visit!

I got in touch with a local garden designer on Instagram who agreed to act as a guide. The next morning, I took a small, six-person

propeller plane from Boston to Nantucket Memorial—a lovely little airport.

After picking up a rental car, I drove to the hotel. Shortly after, my guide showed up. She was a tremendous help, introduced me to a lot of people on the island, and accompanied me to several gardens. It was a fantastic trip, complete with unusually pleasant late summer weather. I visited and photographed a lot of beautiful places. Sadly, none of the Nantucket gardens found their way into this book. They didn't quite have the style and ambience I had seen in pictures, mainly due to it not being rose

season, but also because some of the plants were wilting due to a sweltering summer. Nonetheless, the trip was a dream come true for me.

Three days after landing on the island, I dropped off the car and took the ferry to New Bedford on the mainland. Next stop was Hollister House Garden, roughly a three-hour drive from New Bedford and 150 miles north of New York, and a "Garden Study Weekend" with several people I had met on Instagram. It was a fantastic few days. I met Bunny Williams and Martha Stewart, among others. As it turned out, both already followed me on Instagram.

I was invited to visit their gardens, both of which were about an hour's drive from Hollister House. The next day, Martha Stewart's head gardener showed me around her garden. Next, I headed to Bunny Williams's garden, which turned out to be one of the highlights of my trip.

Follow Bunny on Instagram: @bunnys_eye.

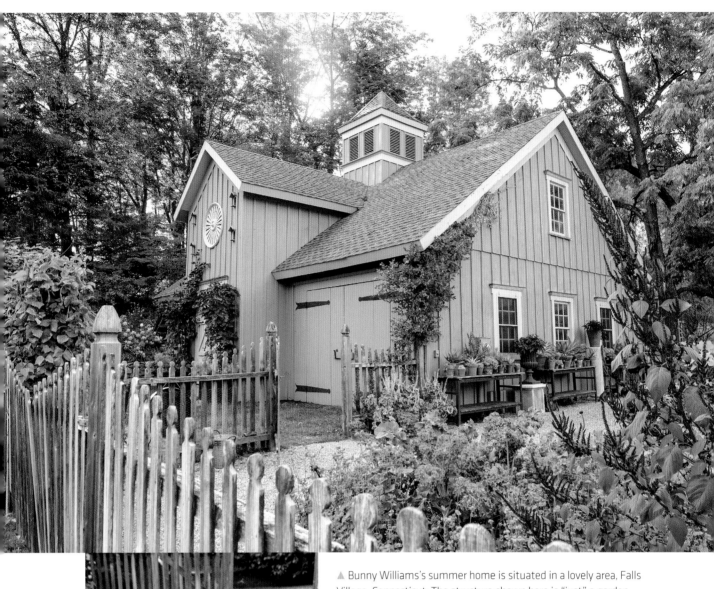

▲ Bunny Williams's summer home is situated in a lovely area, Falls Village, Connecticut. The structure shown here is "just" a garden building next to her kitchen and cutting garden. Bunny's actual house is a charming nineteenth-century manor house that she and her husband, John Rosselli, bought over forty years ago. Try googling "Bunny Williams's garden"—I promise it'll be worth it!

◄ Williams's book *An Affair with a House* (2005) recounts the tale of the restoration and renovation of the house and how the garden took shape. It was my first encounter with Bunny and her universe. I was spellbound.

◄ Bunny uses many classic features in her garden, which she and her husband—both antique dealers—pick up on trips, especially to Europe. The couple have always had an eye for garden antiques, such as this plant theater.

▶ Pots with frost-sensitive plants are dotted around the garden. They are moved into the heated greenhouse before the frost arrives.

▶ Bunny saw a fence like the one framing the garden here at an antiques fair. It consisted of just a single gate and a couple of pickets. She bought them and asked a local carpenter to make fences and gates to match.

◄ Williams is extremely multitalented and one of America's best-known and most respected designers and interior architects. Among other things, she designed this outstanding building next to the kitchen and cutting garden. The starting point for it was the local building style, but she was also greatly inspired by Scandinavian design, Swedish in particular. John is a big fan of the Gustavian style, which has several similarities to the French Louis XVI style but is a little less ornate.

A New England Garden   123

▲ Every winter, Bunny diligently studies seed catalogs and decides which summer flowers to sow in the spring. She loves spending time in the garden but leaves the actual sowing and transplanting to her gardeners.

◀ Amaranth (*Amaranthus cruentus*) is a favorite she plants every season. As an annual, she has to sow it every spring. Some types have upright blooms, while others have hanging, "tail-like" ones. Bunny likes both.

▲ As she showed me around her garden, I was enormously impressed by the breadth and depth of her knowledge, not just about garden design but also about plants. I absolutely loved hearing her thoughts and ideas. We talked about gardens we have both visited, poring over the details of their design, style, and ambience. It was a pleasure to learn that we know many of the same people. Bunny was a key figure in the rest of my New England journey. She is incredibly generous when it comes to sharing her contacts. As it turns out, her name opens all sorts of doors—it's always good to know someone who knows someone.

▼ The big greenhouse is insulated and kept frost-free in winter. New England winters are often long and cold, with lots of snow.

▲ *Amaranthus cruentus*, 'Oeschberg', is a deep purple-red amaranth with rather dark foliage and erect "tails."

▶ Black-eyed Susan (*Rudbeckia hirta* 'Sahara') has beautiful red, orange-yellow, and apricot-colored flowers. It is exceedingly popular because the flowers look so good in bouquets.

◀ Bunny designed the plant supports herself. It almost goes without saying that there are no "off-the-shelf solutions" in her garden. Notice how lettuce is planted out at the bottom of the bed. The ground will soon be covered.

▲ Dahlia 'Happy Days Yellow' is especially beautiful due to its dark foliage, making the yellow flowers stand out and almost shine. It's evident from Bunny's designs that she loves color and is an expert in how to use it, which is why her garden contains flowers in all sorts of colors and shades.

▲ Bunny loves to furnish her garden with pillars and tables for pots. She spends hours arranging her garden and finds it very therapeutic. Despite her age, she continues to be highly active and constantly travels the world. She still works in the company office in New York, where she and John spend winters. As soon as the weather improves, she "escapes" New York and heads 160 miles north to Falls Village.

▲ John also enjoys puttering about in the garden, especially with the vegetables, since he's the one who does the cooking. New England summers are quite balmy, so it's pretty easy to grow tomatoes outdoors.

◀ When Bunny plans a flower bed, she thinks not just in terms of color but also shape and structure. She is particularly fond of foliage and leaves—which is why she loves artichokes, for example. She likes to use their decorative, winged leaves in her big floral arrangements. To prevent the plants from sending out stems and flowering, Bunny doesn't sow the seeds until April/May. That way, she gets the most beautiful foliage.

A New England Garden

▲ The common zinnia (*Zinnia elegans*) is a summer flower and an absolute must for Bunny every year. It's an essential part of her bouquets. Her gardeners plant it in the greenhouse in March and move it out into the garden in May. You can sow it at the growing site, but using a greenhouse gives it a head start. There are many, many fine varieties in pretty much every conceivable color.

▶ When choosing seeds, Bunny tries to meet both her own need for flowers and John's for vegetables. Sometimes, one plant satisfies them both, like this runner bean with orange flowers. It is called *Phaseolus coccineus*, also known as 'Lady Di', after Diana, Princess of Wales. The bright scarlet flowers are followed later by lovely green beans up to 10 to 12 inches (25 to 30 cm) in length.

◀ A few years ago, Bunny commissioned a local carpenter to make this beautiful bench, based on a traditional design.

▶ When *Zinnia elegans* thrives, it can be up to about 3 feet (1 m) tall. It likes to be warm but not too wet.

▶▶ The numerous garden seats give the place a relaxed air and a personal touch. Note the potted ferns.

▲ This must be a strong contender for the world's most beautiful hen house. Bunny designed and gifted it to her husband as a birthday present a few years ago. The two adjacent buildings—a feed house and laying house—are linked to an octagonal chicken coop, which has top-to-bottom netting. The net continues almost 3 feet (1 m) below ground to avoid unwanted visits by burrowing foxes and other hungry predators.

◀ Few people would go to such effort to house chickens—but just look at the beautiful buildings on either side. Both of them would make great garden sheds.

I had a great day with Bunny and John. Hearing Bunny talk about her design principles was highly instructive. It's all about creating spaces, things to see and do and—not least—surprises. It's really important that the whole garden isn't visible all at once. Every time you round a corner, something new awaits. But the varied styles mustn't clash or go off on different tangents. You have to maintain a link between the buildings, fences, and hedges. Once the framework is in place, you can start experimenting with the individual plants and how they fit in with each other. That's the part that fills Bunny with the most joy.

After my visit to Falls Village, I drove north, enjoying the first soft glow of fall on the trees. I ended up in Maine and visited a lot of lovely places, people, and gardens along the way, all of which I will return to in a future book.

For now, it's time to head back to Europe.

Anita's Country Cottage

Anita Bons from the small German town of Wolfenbüttel, about 50 miles (80 km) southeast of Hanover, is another of the many garden friends I have made on Instagram (@mycountrycottage). I was delighted when she agreed to be in this book. My expectations were sky high when I visited her in July 2017 for the first time. I wasn't disappointed. What a paradise!

Anita proves it's possible to have a dream cottage garden in an ordinary residential neighborhood. She grew up in a house with a garden but had no interest in plants. Her interest was sparked in her early thirties when she and Jörg moved into an apartment with a large balcony. She found numerous sources of inspiration online, and things really started to take off. She bought lots of gardening books and magazines, and soon her balcony was stuffed with potted plants. Her longing for a garden grew.

In late summer 2004, Anita and Jörg moved into a newly built house on a flat, approximately 900-square-yard (750-sq m) plot with rich clay soil. She spent the fall and winter of 2004 and the early months of 2005 fixing up the house and working on a plan for the garden. Shortly before moving in, they had sown the grounds with *Phacelia esculentum*, which improves the soil, helping make clay-rich soil lighter and airier. It's called a "green manure plant" because it binds useful nitrogen that benefits the soil. Once they have flowered, the plants are dug up or milled into the ground to release nitrogen—nature's own fertilizer.

On March 29, 2005, they set about tilling the *Phacelia* into the ground. Anita remembers the date because they celebrate the garden's birthday every year!

Next, they sank poles into the ground, stretched out string markers, and planted hedges. While Jörg was laying paving stones, Anita planted lots of roses.

The couple spend their weekends and holidays visiting other people's gardens—not just in Germany but also in the Netherlands—which have served as rich sources of inspiration.

One place from which Anita has derived a host of great ideas, especially when it comes to alliums, is the Mutter-Tochter-Garten (see pages 154–193).

It's great that Anita and I have similar tastes in gardens. She often tells me about the ones she and Jörg visit. If Anita recommends it, I know it's definitely worth a visit.

I really value our gardening friendship. Anita and Jörg have also been to my garden. I went to see them several times to take pictures for this book. It's always nice to go back.

Follow Anita on Instagram:
@mycountrycottage.

▲ There are several highlights in Anita's garden, but her favorite month is May, when the tulips are in full bloom. The color scheme here is tight, with no warm tones (e.g., reds, yellows, and oranges).

The garden is quite intimate and closed off, but you can get a glimpse of paradise from the road, as many passersby do. People often stop for a chat when they see Anita in the garden, usually expressing great admiration for her work but also saying it must be a huge job. There's no doubt about that—but Anita always finds time for a chat and to tell you how much joy her garden brings.

◀ Bleeding heart (*Lamprocapnos spectabilis*) is indispensable.

▲ In May, the front garden is dominated by violet, lilac, and purple. The dark tulip is one of the most popular varieties, 'Queen of Night'. The other two are in shades of lilac ('Recreado') and light violet ('Shirley'). The latter changes quite dramatically during its life cycle. The bud is almost white, with a faint violet edge. As it emerges, it changes color from white to violet. It looks very elegant.

▶ 'Recreado', in the foreground, tends to return several years in a row, as does 'Queen of Night'. Unfortunately, this is not the case with all tulips. Some only bloom for a single season, so enjoy them while you can.

Anita's Country Cottage   135

▲ ◄ Using climbing plants on walls and fences adds to the lushness of the garden. Clematis is a particular favorite. You need to cut late-flowering species back before spring, but not this early-flowering clematis, *Clematis montana* 'Rubens'. It blossoms on top of last year's growth.

► The lavender-colored Cusick's camass (*Camassia cusickii*), is a delicate and discreet bloom. It is particularly popular in the Netherlands. There are also dark-blue and creamy-white varieties.

▼ These beautiful pots with lids are used for forcing rhubarb.

▶ The lilac, *Syringa vulgaris* 'Katherine Havemeyer', has adorable lavender-blue flowers and an intense, lovely scent. All *Syringa vulgaris* varieties have a fantastic fragrance.

▼ Another classic tulip, 'White Triumphator'.

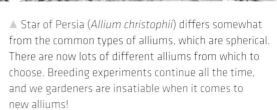

▲ Star of Persia (*Allium christophii*) differs somewhat from the common types of alliums, which are spherical. There are now lots of different alliums from which to choose. Breeding experiments continue all the time, and we gardeners are insatiable when it comes to new alliums!

◄ Canterbury bells (*Campanula medium*) is another of the many types of bellflower. This variety has a classic cottage-garden look but isn't that common for some reason—maybe because it's a biennial and dies back after flowering. The first year after sowing, biennials form evergreen leaves and don't flower until the following year.

▼ Lupins and alliums make a great team, with the tall, colorful spires and spherical blooms contrasting each other wonderfully. A well-balanced garden isn't just about colors—shapes are important too.

◄ In the wild, peach-leaved bellflower (*Campanula persicifolia*) is mainly found in the bright deciduous forests of central Europe. But it is pretty easy to grow in the garden, especially in fairly clay-rich soil.

▲ One of the most impressive alliums is 'Ambassador', which features hundreds of flowers gathered together in a massive ball. The first time Anita saw this variety was in Silke and Elisabeth's garden, Mutter-Tochter-Garten. 'Ambassador' is also notable because it blooms a bit later than the more common *Allium aflatunense* 'Purple Sensation', which flowers in the second half of May and fades in mid-June when 'Ambassador' is ready to take over.

▶ Another bellflower variant, *Campanula persicifolia* 'Alba'. Both the white and the blue grow sporadically. Sowing perennials requires a little patience because it sometimes takes a couple of years—or more—before any flowers grow. The narrow-leaved bellflower blooms the second year after sowing.

▲ Rhubarb plants bloom when they are a few years old. The 3-foot-high (1-m) stems with white flowers look hugely impressive. The problem is that the flowers suck strength from the plant, which stops it from producing a lot of leaves and stems, so many people remove them. Anita lets the flowers grow because she finds them beautiful.

◄ Honesty (*Lunaria annua*) has beautiful flowers but also attractive seedheads that emerge later in the season. In the past, dried seedheads were used for decorative purposes. Given the upsurge in the popularity of dried flowers, honesty may be in for a renaissance.

▽ A sweet and practical idea. The pots are on top of pointed bamboo sticks and other supports for safety reasons, but Anita also writes the names of the plants on the pots when she plants her dahlia bulbs. Anita found an old ladder at a flea market, painted it gray, and uses it as storage space and for displaying potted horned violets.

△ No cottage garden is complete without columbine!

▽ When allium finish flowering, the decorative green seedheads remain. This is the white-flowering variety 'Mount Everest'.

▲ During the planning phase, Anita decided to plant boxwood hedges. She started with small cuttings she had made herself. Today, the hedges are dense and exquisite.

◄ A small insect hotel made by Jörg. If you're thinking of making your own, there are plenty of instructions and suggestions online.

► Jörg designed the decorative hangers for pots based on an idea Anita had seen in a magazine.

▼ In the old days, beehives were made of straw. Some still are and can be used to capture swarms from trees. You hold the straw hive open and shake the tree until the swarm descends into it. As soon as the queen is in, the rest will stay. You then place the straw hive close to where the bees were captured, and any not enticed at first will make their way toward the queen through a small entrance at the bottom. Once all the bees are in—and have calmed down!—they can be transferred to a permanent hive.

◀ Hydrangea (*Hydrangea arborescens*) 'Annabelle', is undoubtedly one of the most popular white hydrangeas. It is especially beautiful when the flowers are in bud, at which point they are lime green.

▼ At the end of the house is a shaded bed with many fine hostas and sedums, both of which are low-maintenance plants.

Childhood Memories

This old farmhouse, 12 miles (20 km) west of Nyborg, Denmark, is the home of another fantastic Danish garden. It fits in beautifully with the surrounding rolling landscape and has a charming, natural cottage-garden style.

Mette Jensen and her husband, Claus, bought the property in the mid-1990s. Mette has been fond of plants and flowers since she was little. She served her apprenticeship as a gardener specializing in breeding plants, which involves using a brush to transfer pollen from one flower's stamens to those of another—a task that requires real patience. Fortunately, she has a lovely garden in which to do this painstaking work.

In this region of Denmark, many people work in horticulture. Even those not personally involved have friends and family who work in the industry. Claus sells plants wholesale and over the years has worked with many different types—tulips, herbs, greenery, and, most recently, dried flowers. The island of Funen is home to many nurseries, albeit fewer than in years gone by.

Mette has always loved gardens and flowers and has fond memories of her paternal grandmother's garden, where she spent many holidays and weekends as a child. She and her grandmother and grandfather would pick flowers, gather berries, and tend the garden.

Mette says that it was a true cottage garden. It didn't matter whether the colors matched— the key consideration was lushness. And lush it was—both in the huge kitchen garden and in the flower and perennial garden. There were countless peonies and sweet peas with the most wonderful scent. Mette recalls that she was allowed to pick as many as she wanted.

When Mette and Claus bought the property, there wasn't much garden here—it was mostly grass. There were chickens, though. The chickens are still here, but their run has been revamped, and the garden has changed quite a bit.

Some years after Mette started her own garden, Isabella Smith opened her mail-order

business selling interesting seeds and bulbs. Mette found this incredibly inspiring. This was before the internet, and Isabella was selling flowers in colors Mette had never seen before—at that time, you couldn't buy sweet peas in a single color, only in mixed batches.

Much has happened since then, and Mette still keeps up to date. Claus frequently visits horticultural shows abroad and brings plants and flowers home to his wife. He knows what she likes. Mette is a romantic soul, so he'll never go wrong with pink, white, lilac, and purple.

Childhood Memories 145

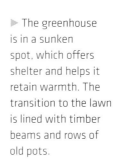

▲ About fifteen years ago, Mette dreamt of a greenhouse, but with three children, spending lots of money on the garden was out of the question. So she was overjoyed to find this one in the classified ads for the equivalent of just $75. A man had bought it a few years earlier, but his grand plans never got off the ground. A shame for him, but a stroke of luck for Mette!

▶ The greenhouse is in a sunken spot, which offers shelter and helps it retain warmth. The transition to the lawn is lined with timber beams and rows of old pots.

▲ Split-level gardens always look good. When Mette and Claus first moved in, the slope was relatively steep, so they embraced it and excavated a sunken garden. They covered the ground with wood chips and now have a little patio decorated with groups of pots. The greenhouse stands on large concrete slabs that provide a solid foundation.

▶ Greenhouses make good space dividers, and you can arrange pots and other garden paraphernalia decoratively along the walls.

A "chestnut fence" like the one seen in the background is a simple way of generating a cottage-garden atmosphere. This one also serves the practical function of keeping the family's two dogs in and the local deer out. In the foreground is *Geranium oxonianum* 'Rose Clair'. Behind it, garden lady's mantle (*Alchemilla mollis*). The stemmed rose is 'Bonica'.

There is something exceptionally pure and beautiful about the white foxglove. However, if you take seeds from it, you can't be sure that the offspring will be white, as foxgloves crossbreed.

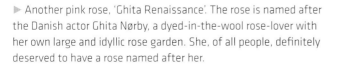 Annual clary (*Salvia viridis*) is a summer flower that Mette sows every spring. It looks great in bouquets. You can buy it in bags of mixed seeds—in pink, white, and blue—or in separate colors. These colored varieties are 'Pink Sunday', 'White Swan', and 'Blue Denim'. The brightly colored parts aren't flowers, though—they're special leaves called bracts. The flowers themselves are tiny and elusive.

▶ Another pink rose, 'Ghita Renaissance'. The rose is named after the Danish actor Ghita Nørby, a dyed-in-the-wool rose-lover with her own large and idyllic rose garden. She, of all people, definitely deserved to have a rose named after her.

▲ It wouldn't be summer without sweet pea (*Lathyrus odoratus*). It is not a surprise that Mette is particularly fond of the variety called 'Solstice Soft Pink'. Some people find sweet peas tricky and have trouble getting the seeds to germinate. I haven't had that problem myself—I've always found them pretty easy to work with, especially if you cultivate them in advance.

◄ Garden phlox (*Phlox paniculata*) is an easy perennial that thrives in most places, so there's every reason to plant it. There's a huge number of varieties. This one is called 'Edentuin'.

▲ There are many new varieties of purple coneflower (*Echinacea purpurea*) these days. Most have a double structure, which makes them spectacular and decorative. The downside is that they're not particularly hardy at northern latitudes. The old-fashioned variety 'Magnus' will thrive in a sunny spot as long as it doesn't have to compete with surrounding plants.

▼ Mette likes chickens. As mentioned, a group of them came with the house, and the couple has kept chickens ever since. They spend most of their time in the coop, but they also love to roam the garden. They are allowed to roam from time to time but mainly in the off-season, when a little havoc in the beds isn't the end of the world.

▲ *Cosmos bipinnatus*, commonly called garden cosmos or Mexican aster, was also found in old cottage gardens. It has always been popular because it produces so many flowers for bouquets. Mette often chooses the good old 'Gloria' variety for its shimmering pink tones. The good thing about this plant is that if you diligently cut the flowers, new ones will constantly appear. This also prevents them from self-seeding.

The Mother-Daughter Garden

In the countryside just outside Bedburg-Hau, about 50 miles (80 km) northwest of Essen, Germany, and not far from the border with the Netherlands, is a unique place known to many German garden lovers. The Mutter-Tochter-Garten (the Mother-Daughter Garden) is owned by Elisabeth Imig and her daughter Silke Imig-Gerold. Over the years, they have become good gardening friends of mine, and they give me a warm welcome every time I visit. Elisabeth and I communicate well enough, even though her English is not great, and my German is even worse. Gesticulation and Latin plant names help.

Born in 1943, she has been interested in gardening for as long as she can remember. As a mere ten-year-old, she had her own bed in her parents' garden. Elisabeth married in 1966 and had two children, Silke being the older.

When they married, she and her husband took over his parents' farm, including its many cows. At the time, her mother-in-law was running the place, after being widowed four years earlier.

As was the custom back then, the farm had a very large kitchen garden with just a few flowers. That all changed when Elisabeth came along. Bit by bit, parts of the kitchen garden, to the mother-in-law's great surprise, were converted into perennial beds, a rare sight at that time. But Elisabeth was highly driven and came up with her own unique style. Most of the plants she sowed herself or obtained via swaps. As money was tight, it was important to make the most of whatever was available. And she did. She still had a relatively large kitchen garden, so the family was largely self-sufficient in food.

In 1985, Elisabeth's husband died. Naturally, she was devastated to find herself a widow at such a young age, and she shut down the farm. Some years later, her mother-in-law also died. It was a difficult period, but she is a remarkably strong woman, and the garden helped her navigate her grief.

Elisabeth has passed on to her daughter the joy of gardening she inherited from her own mother. In 1999, Silke and her husband moved into the renovated cowshed, which became the childhood home for their three children. Once again, three generations of the family were

living under the same roof. The children have now left home, which means Silke has more time for the garden. But she often notes that without her mother and brother, Jens, it simply would not work. This is a strong family, and they pull together.

Elisabeth is in the garden from early morning until late in the evening. After work, Silke and Jens lend a hand, and they often all garden together on the weekends. With no outside help, it is unbelievable how well Silke and Jens look after the approximately 3,500-square-yard (3,000-sq m) garden.

Several times a week during the garden season, enthusiasts pour off buses that arrive from Germany and the Netherlands and all over Europe. There have even been groups from the United States and Japan. Elisabeth conducts the tours, and her love of the garden is infectious. Everybody feels it, even if they don't speak German.

Several books about the garden have also been published, and it has been featured on television. Try searching YouTube for "Mutter-Tochter-Garten."

▼ In 2019 alone, I visited Silke and Elisabeth five times during the garden season—once a month between April and August.

◀ An early morning in April. The morning mist lingered, and hoar frost was visible on the grass. Everything seemed untouched and pristine. A new garden season had just begun.

▼ April is the daffodil month, and there are so many different ones in the garden. This beautiful variety, with the orange center, is called 'Verger'.

▲ The first sight that met me in the early morning light was the circle of daffodils (see the main picture on the previous page). Seen here are a number of varieties, including 'Geranium', 'Verger', and 'Serola'. The last of the three, with its cold yellow petals and orange corona, is an old variety that flowers well.

◀ The garden seating is mostly for guests, as neither Silke nor Elisabeth have much time to sit and ponder. They enjoy the garden while working in it.

▶ The ostrich fern (*Matteuccia struthiopteris*) is so graceful when the leaves unfold.

The Mother-Daughter Garden   157

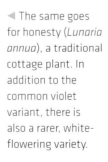

▲ No empty spaces! Even as early as April, the ground is completely covered. Large rosettes of foxgloves, as seen in the middle of the picture, help to fill the gaps. Forget-me-nots (*Myosotis sylvatica*) are also visible. All of them self-seed, thanks to Elisabeth's careful choice of plants many years ago.

◀ The same goes for honesty (*Lunaria annua*), a traditional cottage plant. In addition to the common violet variant, there is also a rarer, white-flowering variety.

▶ It's easy to find the watering can . . . !

▲ The short, early-flowering tulips 'Purple Prince', 'White Prince', and 'Candy Prince' look good together and work well alongside the yellow, cream, and white daffodils.

▶ Silke and Elisabeth both have a penchant for purple and violet tulips. The purple 'Negrita' and the light 'Shirley', in shimmering violet shades, match each other nicely.

▼ It's not spring unless there are pansies. The variety here is 'Pink Shade'. The garden has many features for guests to pause and take in.

▶ The daffodils 'Geranium' and 'Serola' bloom at the same time as the early tulips. The great thing about daffodils is that they are so faithful and come back year after year. Unfortunately, this is not the case with tulips. If the daffodils start to flower less vigorously, dig up the clumps and separate and replant the bulbs individually, around 2.5 to 5 inches (5 to 10 cm) apart. This will reinvigorate them.

The Mother-Daughter Garden   159

▲ Summer snowflake (*Leucojum aestivum*) looks like spring snowflake (*Leucojum vernum*). As the genus name suggests, they are also related. The summer version has similar white, bell-shaped hanging flowers on slender stems.

◀ One of the most beloved small spring bulbs is the grape hyacinth (*Muscari armeniacum*), which comes in several varieties. Shown here is a mix of 'Blue Magic', 'Ocean Magic', and 'White Magic'.

▶ An image like this really makes you yearn for spring. It's so wonderful when the garden wakes up after a long and dark winter. The little white narcissus is called 'Thalia'.

▼ Forget-me-not (*Myosotis sylvatica*) has small flowers and small leaves, which is probably how it got its Latin name—*Myosotis* means mouse ears.

◀ It was only a few years ago that I first encountered this delicate little lavender-blue perennial, Virginia bluebell (*Mertensia virginica*) online. I ordered root stalks and planted them in my own garden in the fall. I was so happy when they flowered in May.

▲ Originally, there was a kitchen garden here. This is excellent, fertile, arable land, where most things will grow, especially roses and perennials. Everything is thriving in this photo.

◀ Mediterranean spurge (*Euphorbia characias*) 'Wulfenii' is found in many European gardens. I have tried in vain to grow it in my garden in Denmark, but it can't cope with our winters. Or perhaps our soil is too moist. It's strange really, considering the relative proximity to Silke and Elisabeth's garden.

▲ At the bottom of the garden is the kitchen area. Elisabeth loves flowers, but she also can't be without her herbs. Although not very big, the kitchen garden provides a reasonably large yield of potatoes, strawberries, radishes, lettuce, string beans, and various cabbages.

▶ Outside Elisabeth's part of the house is a cozy seating area where guests are served coffee. The hares on the table were there because it was Easter, which is a popular holiday for the Germans. Many people hang colored Easter eggs in the trees—but not Silke and her mother. The flowers provide all the decoration they could wish for.

▲ When I visited in May, the tulips were in full bloom. The garden was rich with color, dominated by purples, violets, and pinks. The pink tulip is called 'Mistress'. In the main picture on the previous page, it is seen beside the purple 'Negrita'. Every year, Silke and Elisabeth plant around ten thousand new tulip bulbs. They give it their all.

◀ The dark 'Ronaldo' and pink 'Mistress' also work beautifully together.

▶ 'Fancy Frills' is a pink-to-rose-colored tulip with a fringed edge.

▶ Visitors in May are awestruck by the pink-blossoming kousa dogwood (*Cornus kousa*) 'Sweetwater'. It usually has white flowers, but this variety is an exception. Beginning the second half of May, the tree is covered in beautiful flowers, which sit individually on raised stalks, slightly above the branches. The tree grows quite slowly, and it can easily take five or six years before the first flowers appear (see also the picture on page 164).

▼ 'Chinatown' is a beautiful, very special tulip with green and pink flowers and a decorative white border along its green leaves.

▲ In May, the earliest alliums, *Allium aflatunense* 'Purple Sensation', come into bloom and perfectly match the overall color scheme. As anyone familiar with alliums knows, one downside is that the green leaves quickly become a bit sad looking. It's therefore a really good idea to plant the bulbs between perennials, which—as here—hide the drab foliage.

◄ In a sheltered bed out by the open fields are many lilacs in shades of violet and purple. This dark variety, 'Ludwig Späth', is a classic.

► The garden also has an abundance of columbine.

▶ One person's weed is another's garden masterpiece—for example, cow parsley or wild chervil (*Anthriscus sylvestris*). It blooms in ditches and meadows in the wild in Europe, but some of us have invited it into our gardens. Elisabeth and I completely agree that its light white screens make for a lovely plant—not only in beds but also in bouquets.

◀ 'Louvre' is the name of this lilac and violet tulip. A beautiful variety but not one you see very often.

▼ *Clematis montana* is an early flowering species. The best-known variety is the rose-colored 'Rubens', while 'Mayleen' veers more towards pink.

The Mother-Daughter Garden   169

◀ Presprouted potatoes are put into the ground in late April and are seen here in mid-May, already well on their way. Elisabeth grows several varieties but is nowhere near as self-sufficient in potatoes as her mother-in-law was.

▶ Red campion (*Silene dioica*) lights up the garden with its pink flowers. A prolific self-seeder, it is somewhat impractical here, close to the kitchen garden, so Elisabeth cuts it back or simply pulls it up before the seeds have a chance to spread.

▲ The garden doesn't have a lawn, but facing the open fields is a grassy walkway and a larger space with a couple of lounge chairs. These are more decorative than practical, but visitors occasionally linger here and soak up the idyllic atmosphere. The garden is open one Sunday per month throughout the season. For more information, see www.imig-gerold.de. Just a few miles from Silke and Elisabeth's garden is another extremely worthwhile destination, Manfred Lucenz and Klaus Bender's garden, which is usually open on the same Sundays (see www.lucenz-bender.de). These two gardens alone are definitely worth a trip. They are also close to the Netherlands, which is home to so many fascinating gardens.

▲ With its overhanging growth and drooping flowers, Solomon's seal (*Polygonatum multiflorum*) is a stunning plant. It is often found in deciduous forests, and I have seen it growing wild in Denmark on numerous occasions. It is a prolific plant that puts out a lot of shoots but never becomes invasive. Instead, it prefers to stay in one spot and over time forms a nice big group. And it is very welcome to do so!

▲ *Anthriscus sylvestris* is in the borderland between the kitchen garden and the flower garden. Both Silke and Elisabeth are deeply fond of all varieties of umbellifers—except maybe ground elder/ goutweed (*Aegopodium podagraria*)! Wild chervil is the umbellifer that blooms first. Later comes wild carrot, which also has delicate white flowers. Wild parsnips with lime-yellow flowers follow. Dill and perennial fennel are also worth mentioning here, with their lime-yellow-to-green umbels.

◄ Shallots in rows. These are a mainstay. Elisabeth's mother-in-law grew an incredible number of different vegetables here, especially during World War II.

▶ The allium 'Violet Beauty' is a fairly new variety. Elisabeth likes new plants. In late summer, she studies the bulb catalogs carefully and feeds her enthusiasm.

▼ *Anthriscus sylvestris* 'Ravenswing' is a highly elegant breed of common wild chervil (cow parsley) with dark foliage. Elisabeth uses it in big bouquets, which she arranges in old jam jars. She has a natural talent for it.

The Mother-Daughter Garden   173

▲ June is rose time, and there is an abundance of them here. Since she first heard about them many years ago, Elisabeth has always liked Austin roses, and adds new ones every year. As you wander around the garden, it is obvious that her roses are doing exceptionally well, possibly because she fertilizes them regularly. The impressive climbing rose above the bench at the end of the garden path is 'Francis E. Lester'.

▶ There's something downright majestic about delphiniums standing tall and proud in the garden. They used to be quite a regular sight, especially in cottage gardens, but pop up a bit less often nowadays, which is a pity. The most common varieties are blue, but this one, 'Sweethearts', is rose-colored.

◀ Lady's mantle (*Alchemilla mollis*) has self-seeded in the gravel path. Sometimes self-seeders can be a little too enthusiastic. To stop them from spreading, cut the plants right back before the seeds develop. That way, you also get fresh new foliage.

▶▶ Valerian (*Valeriana officinalis*) stands tall above the roses. See pages 178–179 for further info.

▲ Height is a challenge with delphiniums. They can easily topple over or break during a storm or heavy rainfall. The trick is to support them before things go wrong (e.g., with bamboo or branches).

◀ Big betony (*Stachys grandiflora*) 'Superba' is a low-maintenance, unpretentious perennial.

▶ The color of the 'Rhapsody in Blue' rose makes it a clear favorite. Especially at this stage, when the flowers have not fully opened, the purple hue is deep and intense. It softens somewhat as it opens up.

▲ Some people say peonies stop flowering if you move them—but that's not quite the whole story. It may take a season or two before they bloom again, but they will have "a second childhood." In an older plant, the root stalks will be pretty big. Use a spade to divide them. Replant the pieces by placing them with the buds ('eyes') facing up and covering them with just a few inches of soil. If planted too deep, they will not flower. The one above is the pink 'Bowl of Beauty'.

▶ *Rosa rugosa* 'Roseraie de l'Hay' is a cultivated beach rose with full pink flowers. Normally, *Rosa rugosa* spreads widely through its root system, but this is not a problem with the cultivated varieties, which are grafted to non-spreading roots. If you see one at the nursery or garden center, it's a good idea to check that it is grafted.

◀ The peony 'Jan van Leeuwen' is a characteristic white variety with distinctive yellow stamens.

▶ A self-seeded delphinium. This perennial is not usually a keen self-seeder, but in places where it thrives, you may be lucky. The biggest problem is that they are often crowded out.

The Mother-Daughter Garden   177

◀ ▲ The poppy is a classic cottage plant. I previously mentioned the perennial poppy (*Papaver orientale*) and the full peony poppy (*Papaver somniferum*), which is an annual. This one is the single-flowered opium poppy (*Papaver somniferum*). It grows here in a swath out towards the open fields and self-seeds year after year.

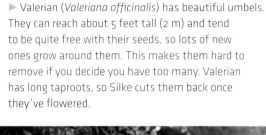

▶ Valerian (*Valeriana officinalis*) has beautiful umbels. They can reach about 5 feet tall (2 m) and tend to be quite free with their seeds, so lots of new ones grow around them. This makes them hard to remove if you decide you have too many. Valerian has long taproots, so Silke cuts them back once they've flowered.

◀ Largest masterwort (*Astrantia maxima*) is a wild species with extra-large flowers. The petals have a delicate hint of mother-of-pearl, making this an especially beautiful accompaniment to the pinkish roses.

▶ Early morning, as the sun comes up, is sheer bliss for a garden photographer. Later, when the sun is high in the sky, it is difficult to take good pictures. You have to wait until the sun starts to go down again.

◀ Great masterwort (*Astrantia major*) comes in many beautiful varieties. This dark red one is called 'Claret'. 'Lars', a Danish variety from the now-closed Lynge Staudegarneri, has even darker flowers.

▶ 'Rosa Mundi' is an heirloom rose with decorative and fragrant two-tone flowers. In late summer, beautiful orange rosehips arrive.

▲ ▶ Most of the beds were previously edged by low boxwood hedges, but an all-too-common fungal disease killed them off. In their place, Silke has planted Japanese holly (*Ilex crenata*), which is a nice evergreen substitute.

▼ Feverfew (*Tanacetum parthenium*) is one of Elisabeth's favorite plants.

The Mother-Daughter Garden   181

▲ Meadow cranesbill (*Geranium pratense*) is often found in the wild in Denmark, even though it is not technically considered Danish flora—it is not a native wild species but one that has strayed from our gardens. It is only wild in the sense that it proliferates rapidly on vacant patches of soil. Standing about 2 feet to 2 feet 4 inches (60 to 70 cm) high, it's quite a tall cranesbill, so it needs support. It is at its best and most beautiful in close symbiosis with other plants, especially roses.

◄ The cranesbill geranium is one of the very best companion plants for roses. The two plants look beautiful entwined like this. This is 'Mary Rose' by David Austin.

◄ 'Angela' is a pink rose that forms a well-shaped and compact shrub with plenty of flowers, which can be seen from a distance.

▶ Another tall cranesbill is 'Patricia', which reaches about 3 feet (1 m) and needs support. This is a prototypical cranesbill with beautiful pink petals and a dark center.

▲ 'Queen of Sweden' is one of Austin's most striking roses of the approximately two hundred absolutely fantastic varieties he bred over six decades. He kept creating wonderful varieties right up until his death at the age of ninety-two in December 2018.

For nearly seventy-five years, David Austin worked tirelessly on roses and introduced his first to the market in 1961. And what a rose it was! 'Constance Spry' (see page 34) is still loved and admired to this day. One of Austin's most famous roses is 'Gertrude Jekyll' (see page 115), which has twice been voted the favorite rose of British enthusiasts.

I'm a big fan of Austin's roses (also known as the English roses), which are among the strongest brands in the plant world. On several occasions, I have visited his company's world-famous rose garden in Shropshire. Each time, it has been a great experience. I was lucky enough to be allowed to park at Austin's private residence beside the garden, which meant I could visit the garden both early in the morning and well into the evening when it was no longer open to the public. A great privilege indeed!

▲ In July, I visited the Mother-Daughter Garden for the fourth time that year. Some of the roses were still in bloom, and there were plenty of hydrangeas, phlox, and the first dahlias. The white hydrangea on the left is *Hydrangea arborescens* 'Annabelle'. This is a classic, seen in a lot of gardens. It grows well in partial shade, which means the flowers last longer. This is true of all hydrangeas.

◀ *Sedum spectabile*, the ice plant, is in my opinion most beautiful when in bud because the whole plant is green. The lovely pink flowers come later.

▶ *Phlox paniculata* 'Blauer Morgen' is one of the bluest phlox.

▲ There are a few hundred hydrangea species, one of the most distinctive being the mountain hydrangea (*Hydrangea serrata*). You can always identify it by the fact that it has two types of flowers—the inflorescence consists of a multitude of very small fertile flowers surrounded by larger, sterile ones. *Hydrangea serrata*, originally from Korea and Japan, is smaller—in terms of both growth and flower size—than the common garden hydrangea. The variety shown here, 'Blue Bird', is one of the most common.

◀ ▲ The most common hydrangea species is *Hydrangea macrophylla*, known simply as garden hydrangea. There are many varieties, and neither Silke nor Elisabeth remember what this particular one is called. Over the years, Elisabeth has taken a number of cuttings, which are planted around the garden and have, over time, grown into quite large shrubs. Interestingly, unlike this one, not all of the flowers are blue. This is due to the soil—acidic conditions produce blue hydrangeas, while calcareous soil results in near-pink ones. It's wonderful!

▼ This garden phlox (*Phlox paniculata*), 'Amethyst', has a beautiful purple-to-pink color that varies with the light.

◄ A particularly fine hollyhock (*Alcea rosea*) with wavy-edged flowers. It is sometimes difficult to identify the variety, because when you take seeds and sow them, you don't know what color flowers will emerge—it's a lottery. If you want to be 100 percent certain of what you'll get, you need to take cuttings.

▲ There is something particularly elegant about small-flowering clematis, such as *Clematis diversifolia* 'Inspiration'. This is a late-flowering clematis with violet-to-pink flowers. It needs to be cut all the way down in early spring at the latest, when it starts to shoot.

▶ The daylily (*Hemerocallis*) 'Ed Murray' is a dark burgundy. It has nothing to do with ordinary lilies, which are bulbous plants. This is a perennial and comes in myriad colors. It's a robust, old-fashioned perennial that likes full sun and produces many flowers.

◀ The climbing rose 'Constance Spry' was David Austin's first variety. It has large, impressive, peony-like heads and a fantastic fragrance.

The Mother-Daughter Garden   187

▲ Kiss-me-over-the-garden-gate (*Polygonum orientale*) reaches quite an impressive height considering it has to start all over again from seed every year. This is an annual summer flower that has to be sown in the fall from fresh seeds; otherwise, it struggles to germinate.

◄ Indian chrysanthemum (*Chrysanthemum indicum*) only starts budding as the days shorten. This is a true fall and winter plant.

▶ Himalayan balsam (*Impatiens glandulifera*).

▲ There is something particularly lovely about the garden in late August, when the summer flowers bloom alongside late-flowering perennials. This is the spider flower (*Cleome hassleriana*) 'Violet Queen'. It also comes in white and pink.

▶ Elisabeth always has flowers on the table and loves to make bouquets, much to the delight of her visitors. One ideal plant for this purpose is love-lies-bleeding (*Amaranthus caudatus*), the drooping growth of which oozes distinctive charm. I personally like to use it in beds, pots, and bouquets, often accompanied by dahlias.

▼ The ice plant (*Sedum spectabile*) is only now beginning to show color. Up to this point, it has been completely green. In the past, it was often found in cottage gardens because it is so easy to propagate. Just stick a shoot in moist soil, and it will quickly take root.

▲ Japanese anemone (*Anemone hupehensis*) 'Praecox' reaches a height of 1 foot 8 inches to ten feet (50 to 60 cm). It is only half as tall as the most common version, *Anemone japonica* (see the next page).

◀ Red bistort or mountain fleece (*Persicaria amplexicaulis*) is a reasonably compact perennial with light flower buds.

▶ The toad lily (*Tricyrtis formosana*) 'Dark Beauty' is another beautiful late-summer perennial.

▲ Lamb's ear (*Stachys byzantina*) is especially beautiful in late summer when the dew settles, and the leaf seems to become even more silvery. This variety, 'Big Ears', has extra-large leaves and almost no flowers.

◄ ▼ The two most common varieties of *Anemone japonica* are the pink 'Königin Charlotte' and the white 'Honorine Jobert'. Both grow to well over 3 feet (1 m) tall.

▲ The beautiful
common zinnia
(*Zinnia elegans*) is
a fantastic summer
flower that Elisabeth
sows in the kitchen
garden every year.

◀ 'Purple Haze', a
long-stemmed dahlia,
is especially well suited
to bouquets. Here it
is in the company of
the upright-flowering
Amaranthus cruentus,
which goes by several
names, including
red amaranth.

◀ The orange flowers appear in Silke and Elisabeth's garden in late summer. Here, the dahlia 'Sylvia' is about to open up. In full bloom, it forms a pompom that I never will tire of looking at—it's just so exquisite.

▶ As mentioned, Elisabeth is a prolific maker of bouquets, but she is also really fond of wreaths. Here is one that she made on the occasion of my visit.

Chocolate Box Cottage

When I showed pictures of this beautiful house and garden to the English hostess at my guest house, she clasped her hands together and excitedly exclaimed, "Oh, a chocolate box cottage!" I hadn't heard the term before and didn't know exactly what it meant, but it was so expressive that I sensed it was highly appropriate.

I later searched the internet for "chocolate box cottage," and a large number of hits appeared on screen, each more charming than the last. I also found a definition. The term originated in the late Victorian era and relates to illustrations on the packaging of Cadbury's chocolate.

One of the most quintessentially English things ever, Cadbury was established in Birmingham in 1824 by John Cadbury (1801–1889). He wanted to make chocolate available to all so that this invigorating foodstuff, which was considered healthy at the time, wasn't the preserve of the rich. He—and later his sons, Richard (1835–1899) and George (1839–1922)—quickly became the largest chocolate producer in England. In 1854, Queen Victoria appointed Cadbury as the official chocolate supplier to the royal family.

The factory grew rapidly and had to move out of the city. In 1878, the two brothers, who had taken over from their father, bought a large piece of land (well over 14 acres) a dozen miles or so south of Birmingham. The following year, they began to build a new factory there, with surrounding large green areas where the factory workers could play tennis, cricket, and soccer or do gymnastics. The Cadbury brothers named the factory and surrounding area Bournville.

In 1893, another 2,550 acres (140 hectares) were purchased near the factory, and over the following years, the brothers built 143 beautiful Arts and Crafts- and Tudor-style houses—all

with an ornamental front garden and a large kitchen garden with fruit trees to the rear. The houses were not built for profit but to offer the factory workers beautiful and functional homes at an affordable price.

Richard Cadbury died in 1899. His loss hit George very hard and made him think about the future. In 1900, he set up the Bournville Village Trust, a foundation that eventually built a total of 313 houses. The creation of the foundation meant that this place, with its generous spirit, would continue even after his death.

However, George soon discovered that people were buying the beautiful houses to sell them at a profit. So, he started building homes

intended solely for renting. These became known as Ten Shilling or Sunshine houses, with affordable rent to help low-income families. Several of them adorned the company's chocolate boxes. Hence the term "chocolate box cottage." Bournville was also the name of Cadbury's dark chocolate bar, which launched in 1908. It is still sold all over the world, as is Dairy Milk, in the famous purple packaging, which hit the market a few years earlier.

The "garden city," as Bournville was called, inspired a movement that eventually reached Denmark. In 1909, F. C. Boldsen visited England to study garden cities and then, in 1912, published a pioneering housing policy proposal.

That same year, he founded the Danish Garden Housing Association, based on the garden city movements in England and Germany. However, the first such projects in Denmark– Præstevangen (1911) and Grøndalsvænge (1912), both in Brønshøj near Copenhagen–were founded independently of the association.

Well, that turned into a long story. But I like good stories and find the chocolate-box tale fascinating.

I love England! Nothing quite beats driving around its small, winding roads, visiting gardens, and talking to the lovely people who live there. Over the years, I have covered thousands of miles and am always on the lookout—especially for signs saying "historic village." That's how I found myself in the Hampshire village of Wherwell. It's a real chocolate-box village, with the most delightful old houses. Search the internet for Wherwell, and you'll see what I mean!

The old convent, Wherwell Priory, dates back to Queen Elfrida in 986. The main building of the stately home dates from around 1820. The area is not only known for its picturesque atmosphere but also for the abundant wild trout in the River Test. This attracts fly fishers from far and wide, including the late U.S. President George H. W. Bush (1924–2018).

On Church Street, which traverses the River Test, lovely little thatched houses stand side by side like pearls on a string, including this beautiful yellow house that caught my eye. Not only was it exceedingly captivating, but also a lot of thought was given to its garden. All of the flowers were white, light yellow, or cream and perfectly matched the yellow-washed brickwork. Various hostas and other leafy plants provided a lush base. I simply had to know more about this place.

Chocolate Box Cottage   197

I rang the bell, and the door was opened by a charming older English gentleman. I explained that I was a garden photographer and author working on a book about cottage gardens. Would it be OK if I took some pictures?

The owner invited me in and asked me to take a seat in the cozy, low-ceilinged living room. He told me that he had become a widower a few years earlier and that his late wife had a green thumb and had designed the garden. Throughout their long marriage, he had helped to look after it, but she was the head gardener, as he put it.

He now took pride in tending it, in tribute to her. The numerous full garden-waste bags at the roadside told me that he'd had the shears out. The man was only too happy to tell me all about the garden and the house.

He said I was welcome to take as many pictures as I liked. When I asked about plant names, he brought out his wife's old notes. They were a great help in finding the names of the roses.

The man was kindness personified but saw no reason for me to use his name. And I respect that, of course. I was delighted by his generous hospitality, and I sensed that he wanted to talk.

He told me that he had not previously fully understood his wife's passion but that he was now all-in on the garden life and often chatted about horticultural matters with other villagers.

Chocolate Box Cottage   199

▲ Clematis 'Marie Boisselot' has large, pure-white flowers that open in early June, at the same time as the roses. In the background is the creamy white Austin rose 'Tranquility'.

▶ In early spring, lungwort (*Pulmonaria officinalis*) 'Sissinghurst White' develops small white flowers. When they wither, the lovely, white-spotted foliage remains.

▲ 'The Pilgrim' is one of the best-known Austin roses. It has beautiful white-yellow flowers with a delicate citrus scent and can be grown as both a shrub and a climbing rose.

◄ Sometimes it's important to make a virtue of necessity. Hydrangea 'Annabelle' grows in and around its iron support (see also the previous page).

▼ 'White Cloud' is another pretty cream-colored rose.

I was also allowed to photograph the big back garden. Among other things, it contains white alliums, 'Mount Everest', which from a distance look like soap bubbles floating over the bed. The owner told me that he added extra bulbs every year, because he found that they eventually stop blooming after a few years. I know the feeling. They are not quite as faithful as, for example, *Allium aflatunense* 'Purple Sensation'.

▶ *Iris germanica* 'White Knight' is a pure-white variety with large, attractive flowers. Here, it is planted all the way from the edge of the bed to the tiled path, where it warms its "feet." It clearly likes this spot and expresses its gratitude with many flowers.

▶ 'Festiva Maxima' is a classic white peony, recognizable by the slight pink tinge on the petals. It has an irresistible scent and impressive flowers.

▲ When thinking about cottage gardens, never forget the common pink (*Dianthus plumarius*). It used to be seen everywhere in these types of small gardens, growing in sunny spots with dry soil. For some reason, it is rarely seen these days, perhaps because it has long been perceived as a funeral flower. The variety here is 'Haytor White'.

▶ When they see a self-seeding plant thriving in an unlikely or random spot, I've heard gardeners say, "It's as if God planted it." Garden lady's mantle (*Alchemilla mollis*) is a prime example. Small surprises like this are particularly welcome in cottage gardens, which are a bit more casual and easygoing.

Chocolate Box Cottage   205

More German Idyll

Although this garden is located in Germany, more precisely Hamburg, the house very much looks like a typical chocolate-box cottage (see pages 194–195).

I found it while searching online for cottage gardens. The website called it Loki-Schmidt-Garten. At the time, I had no idea who Loki Schmidt was, but I very much wanted to see her garden, so I did a bit more research.

I soon discovered that Loki Schmidt (1919–2010) was a well-known environmentalist—in fact, one of the first in Germany. In 1976, she founded Stiftung zum Schutze gefährdeter Pflanzen (Foundation for the Protection of Endangered Plants). The foundation later changed its name to Stiftung Naturschutz Hamburg und Stiftung zum Schutze gefährdeter Pflanzen (Hamburg Nature Conservation Fund and Foundation for the Protection of Endangered Plants).

In 1980, Schmidt set up the Flower of the Year organization, which protects endangered wildflowers in Germany. She also wrote a number of books on subjects including wild plants and nature conservation. Her last book, a complete list of botanical gardens in Germany, was published in October 2010, the month she passed away. Her funeral was a grand affair—almost like a state event.

Schmidt left a huge mark on her country, and almost all Germans over a certain age still know her name. This is partly because for sixty-eight years, she was married to the Social Democratic politician Helmut Schmidt (1918–2015), who was Chancellor of West Germany from 1974 to 1982.

Both she and her husband were from Hamburg. In 2009, she was awarded honorary citizenship of the city. In 2012, two years after her death, Botanischer Garten der Universität Hamburg (Hamburg Botanical Garden), which opened in 1919, was renamed Loki-Schmidt-Garten in her honor. And that's where this gorgeous little farmhouse is located.

I have always liked botanical gardens and have visited a lot of them, but it was still surprising to see an old farm garden here.

It was a little challenging to find information about this lovely little garden, but I was told by the staff that the small farmhouse was built in the early eighties and was at first open to visitors. Since the nineties, it has housed a small shop on weekends.

The garden is laid out according to a plan from the Alter Botanischer Garten in the middle of Hamburg, near the famous flower park Pflanzen und Blumen, which is notable for its old greenhouses, large lake, and delightful ambience.

▲ The garden features both perennials and summer flowers. Sweet pea (*Lathyrus odoratus*) is an obvious choice. There are all sorts of varieties, each more beautiful than the last, and all have a wonderful scent. This lavender-colored variety is called 'Sunshine Light Blue' There are also perennial varieties. The great thing about them is that they come back year after year. But the downside is that they are scentless.

◀ Hollyhocks reach for the sky and self-seed wherever they find space.

▶ *Cosmos bipinnatus*, commonly called the garden cosmos or Mexican aster, is another keen self-seeder—not only in the beds but also on the paths. In this garden, they rake the paths to keep them at bay.

▲ The old baroque gardens feature low boxwood hedges that surround the flower beds and separate them from the neatly laid gravel paths. This way of marking the flower beds was cutting edge among the European upper classes in the seventeenth and eighteenth centuries, but in the nineteenth century, it started to be used in farm gardens too. The beds were planted with cuttings, which you had to acquire yourself, of course, because buying plants was unthinkable back then.

▼ 'Blauer Morgen' is very similar to the famous 'Blue Paradise'. I, for one, have a hard time telling them apart. However, the German breeder Peter zur Linden, from Osnabrücker Staudenkulturen, who introduced 'Blauer Morgen', says the two varieties have nothing to do with each other.

▶ *Phlox paniculata* 'Blue Flame' is another appealing variety, with distinctive, light-blue flowers.

▲ It feels as if the ox-eye daisy (*Leucanthemum vulgare*) has gone out of fashion. Once common in old cottage and peasant gardens, it is rare today. It has a plethora of names, including the dog daisy and marguerite. This wild daisy is found in gravel pits, pastures, arable land, meadows, embankments, and along roadsides, and comes in both new and hybrid garden varieties.

▼ Garden phlox (*Phlox paniculata*) 'Purple Kiss'. No one seems to know quite how many varieties of this beautiful perennial there are—but there are undoubtedly several hundred, perhaps even thousands. And new ones are constantly being added.

▲ The spider flower (*Cleome hassleriana*) 'Violet Queen' grows wild in South and North America.

◄ Another summer flower, Chinese asters (*Callistephus chinensis*) 'Prinova Dark Red'. It comes in a variety of colors and shapes, all of which look great in bouquets.

▲ *Cosmos bipinnatus*, commonly called the garden cosmos or Mexican aster, originated in Mexico, where Spanish monks cultivated it in monastery gardens. Due to its evenly distributed petals, the flower was christened cosmos, which comes from the Greek *kosmos*, meaning world and order.

▶ Although the daisy has fallen out of favor as a garden plant, the opposite is true of the everlasting flower (*Helichrysum bracteatum*). Previously dismissed as a relic of the past, it is now trendier than ever. They make excellent dried flowers, and new and attractive varieties are now appearing in hitherto unseen pastel tones.

▲ Danes call the common evening primrose (*Oenothera biennis*) both "the night light" and—as it was known in my grandparents' West Jutland country garden—the "eight o'clock flower." I remember this quite clearly because my grandmother showed me how it bloomed at eight o'clock in the evening (plus or minus a quarter of an hour). It blossomed all night, only to close and wither away the next day. Pure magic! I have rarely seen this enchanting plant since. If twenty-first-century children want to experience its magic, they will have to wait an extra hour. Modern summertime means that the flowers now come out around nine o'clock.

◀ The yellow perennials 'Cloth of Gold', or yarrow (*Achillea filipendulina*), and dark mullein (*Verbascum nigrum*) also have their origins in the classic farm garden.

▲ ▶ Old paintings of English cottage gardens almost invariably feature delphiniums, with their tall, beautiful spires, densely packed with flowers—predominantly in blue but also white and pink. Some delphiniums are a little more "loose-leafed," like *Delphinium grandiflorum* 'Blue Butterfly', with its vivid blue flowers. This is a relatively short variety, but more interestingly, it can be propagated from seeds. Lots of companies sell the seeds—just take a look online.

The Quintessential Cottage

I think this lovely little English garden with its beautiful house is a quintessential cottage garden. As noted at the beginning of the book, cottage gardens are not exactly found on every street corner—not even in England.

I became aware of Clover Cottage in Cambridgeshire a few years ago when *The English Garden* magazine featured an article about the garden and its owners, Shirley and Paul Shadford. The charming place adorned the cover. Even before I opened the magazine, I knew I had to visit. And I did, a few months later, after I had contacted Shirley, told her about my book project, and asked if I might visit. As you know, gardeners are very nice people, so she kindly agreed.

In mid-June 2018, I drove to West Wickham, a small village 20 miles (32 km) southeast of Cambridge. Here in the middle of the village, down a narrow road, lay Clover Cottage, looking just as it had for nearly three hundred years. I arrived full of excitement and anticipation. As I passed through the gate topped with a climbing rose, I had no doubt that this was the real thing.

Shirley and Paul made tea and kindly told me about their joint project—not only the restoration and renovation of the house but also the creation of the garden, completely from scratch. For Shirley, in particular, it was love at first sight. This was a place where she could create the cottage garden of her dreams. Crucially, the plot was an appropriate size— about a 1,200 square yards (1,000 sq m), neither too big nor too small. The house is right in the middle of the grounds, and at first, Shirley focused on the front garden. She later added a

pond behind the house, complete with water lilies and fish. This was followed by potted plants and cozy seating areas overlooking open fields.

When the couple first moved here, there were only a few trees and virtually no flowers. Shirley saw that as an advantage, because it made it easier to put her own stamp on the place. She not only had the dreams but also the will to bring them to life. She planted roses, clematis, cranesbill, and other hardy, low-maintenance perennials. Delicate plants are not her favorite nor are flowers in bold, warm colors like red and orange. She likes pastels, as well as blue and pink—the traditional colors of old cottage gardens.

During the garden season, Shirley regularly opens the garden to the public. The first time is in February, for a very special reason. At that time of year, the beds are completely white with snowdrops. In one of the first seasons after moving here, she planted hundreds of bulbs arranged in small groups. A few years later, she dug up the groups, divided the bulbs, and replanted. She has been doing this every other year ever since. Now, thousands of snowdrops bloom every winter. Try searching the internet for "Clover Cottage snowdrops." It's a magical sight!

In March, the garden is opened again, because this is when the hellebores (or Lenten roses), dogtooth violets, alpine violets, and other lovely spring plants are in bloom. It then opens again in May and June.

There is a proud tradition of open gardens in England. Many private owners open theirs to the public as part of the National Garden Scheme (NGS), which means that the proceeds go to charity. NGS takes care of the administration, collects the money, and passes it on to medical charities and other good causes. In 2019 alone, the Scheme raised £3 million (about $3.7 million).

Information on open gardens can be found in *The Garden Visitor's Handbook* (formerly called *The Yellow Book*), on the organization's website (ngs.org.uk), or via the app NGS Find a Garden.

◄ ▼ Above the gate, I recognize the climbing rose 'Blush Noisette', with half-filled blue-pink flowers, which I have seen in so many places in England. Although it does grow elsewhere, it seems right at home in England's temperate climate.

The noisette roses were created by the gardening brothers Louis and Philip Noisette. Although they lived in France and the United States, respectively, they collaborated across the Atlantic. Philip often sent seeds of his hybrids to France, where Louis propagated the plants and introduced them to Europe.

This information is from Torben Thim's fantastic book *Historiske Roser* (*Historic Roses*), which is the definitive work on the subject in Danish.

▲ Shirley's garden also features peonies, of course—and once again, the variety is 'Sarah Bernhardt'. So, who was this Sarah Bernhardt who gave her name to both a peony and a cake?

Her full name was Sara-Marie-Henriette Rosine Bernhardt (1844–1923). Bernhardt was the child (born out of wedlock) of a high-class Parisian prostitute and grew up in a convent. As a young woman, she attended drama school. A teacher there was one of her mother's many lovers and a half-brother to Napoleon III.

At thirteen, the young Sarah made her debut on stage and soon gained a reputation for being among the finest dramatic actors ever, earning the nickname the "Divine Sarah." Among other things, she played the title role in *The Lady of the Camellias*.

◄ ▲ The fast-growing climbing rose 'Phyllis Bide' typically takes three seasons before covering an entire arch like this. This rose is an excellent choice for an arch or trellis, because it blooms all the way up the stems and not just at the top. While the half-filled flowers are not that big, there are plenty of them. They alternate between apricot pink and cream.

▲ Both the garden and house are extremely well maintained. The thatched roof is largely new. There are still quite a few thatched houses in England. It is a tradition cherished by the English—which is fortunate, as it's part of the DNA of these old buildings.

▶ Shirley is very fond of cranesbills because they are so easy to work with and very reliable. Here, *Geranium psilostemon* is the star. It is easy to understand why cranesbills were so popular in traditional cottage gardens and are still well-loved to this day. Not many plants are so amenable, with such abundant blooms. It's a low-maintenance flower that will give you no trouble.

◀ The perennial cornflower (*Centaurea montana*) is another classic cottage garden flower with a slightly wild look. It is usually blue but also comes in other colors, including pink, as seen here. This variety is called 'Carnea'.

▲ Earlier in the book, I discussed Geoff Hamilton, the highly respected television host from *Gardeners' World*. After he passed away in 1996, David Austin honored him by naming a rose 'Geoff Hamilton'; with its spherical heads, it is one of the most beautiful roses I've ever seen. I'm sure he was smiling down from heaven when it was launched.

▶ One plant allowed to self-seed around the garden is red valerian (*Centranthus ruber*).

▼ The genus *Thalictrum* is highly prized, not least because of the Chinese meadow rue (*Thalictrum delavayi*) that produces violet-colored flowers in high summer. Here, however, is the greater meadow rue or columbine seed star (*Thalictrum aquilegifolium*), with fine tufted flowers.

▶ The bellflower (*Campanula persicifolia*) 'Alba' is not to be missed.

▶▶ 'Black Knight' is a well-known variety of delphinium, with striking, almost luminous blue flowers tinged with purple. Its relatively slender, upright spires bring a touch of lightness to the bed.

A Beautiful Garden in Southern Sweden

I love Sweden and, in particular, Österlen in the far south, which is home to countless beautiful gardens. I have many good gardening friends in Österlen, which is about an hour's drive from the Øresund Bridge linking Copenhagen and Malmö and is known as Sweden's Provence because the landscape, with its rolling hills and narrow roads winding between rock formations, is reminiscent of the south of France.

The photographs in this section of the book are from Kivik, a small port town to the west, about 60 miles (100 km) from Malmö. The small fishing village dates back to the Middle Ages and is surrounded by charming old fishermen's cottages with lush gardens. The roses here are particularly impressive due to the mild coastal climate.

Not far from the harbor is Kerstin Mannergren Aagren's garden, another place with a classic cottage feel to it.

I got to know Kerstin and her fairytale garden in the 2010s when we were introduced by mutual gardening friends. We hit it off straight away, and visiting her is always a pleasure. Sadly, my visit at the end of August 2019 turned out to be the last. Just after Christmas, I received word from friends that Kerstin had died. I was distraught.

We had spent many a pleasant hour in each other's company. The last time we saw each other, Kerstin had invited me to lunch with friends. Seven of us sat around the table in her little kitchen as she loaded up our plates.

The house is an early nineteenth-century fisherman's cottage, which Kerstin and her husband, Göran, inherited from his parents. At the time, it was a summer home, with fruit trees and berry bushes but few flowers. Kerstin was interested in gardening from an early age. In fact, she had a clear memory of her parents buying a new house when she was about two years old. It was the first time she helped with planting the beds.

Between 1982 and 1985, Kerstin and her husband lived in London, where Göran was the principal of the Swedish School and Kerstin was a teacher. She also taught in high schools in Sweden before and after that, including in English. She loved England and would often talk about how she visited some of its many nurseries and gardens over the years, and how these visits inspired her garden dreams.

Before Kerstin and Göran moved to London, they bought a house in Kristianstad, around 30 miles (50 km) north of the cottage in Kivik. Kerstin had a large garden there and wrote gardening articles for the local newspaper. She was also active in the Rose Society in Scania.

A few years after she was widowed in 2005, Kerstin moved to Kivik, where she loved to putter about in the garden and entertain friends and acquaintances.

After her death, I wondered what would become of Kerstin's beautiful garden. I received an indirect answer when I spoke with her four daughters in January. I wanted to know if it was okay with them that I wrote about their mother and her garden now that she was no longer with us.

They replied, "Of course we want you to write about mum's garden. We think that would be a beautiful way to honor and preserve her memory. She is greatly missed, and we need to get used to her no longer being the center of our family. We will do our best with the garden, but it won't stay the same. So it's good to know that you documented and photographed it at its best."

I was so happy to have their blessing to tell the story of Kerstin and her work, and to hear that they would look after the garden, which will remain a peaceful and beautiful spot for many years to come.

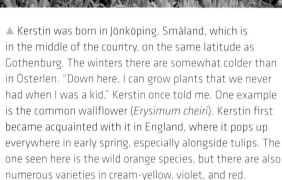

▲ Kerstin was born in Jönköping, Småland, which is in the middle of the country, on the same latitude as Gothenburg. The winters there are somewhat colder than in Österlen. "Down here, I can grow plants that we never had when I was a kid," Kerstin once told me. One example is the common wallflower (*Erysimum cheiri*). Kerstin first became acquainted with it in England, where it pops up everywhere in early spring, especially alongside tulips. The one seen here is the wild orange species, but there are also numerous varieties in cream-yellow, violet, and red.

▼ Forget-me-not (*Myosotis sylvatica*) is a welcome herald of spring. It is notable for its delicate and discreet blue flowers and seems extra beautiful as part of a dense flower canopy among the daffodils and tulips.

▲ Kerstin's house is down a small lane that's almost too narrow for cars. The intimate setting, the beautiful old houses, and the picturesque environment attract plenty of summer tourists, who frequently pause at this gate to marvel at the garden. In the summer, thousands of people visit Österlen, but in the off-season, it's very quiet. Kivik's population is just over a thousand. Over Easter, the number of residents starts to increase, as many Swedes—especially from farther north—have vacation homes in the area. This is when the village springs back to life.

▲ Österlen does not have as many wooden houses as the towns further north (like in Småland). But an old washhouse made of wood gives the garden a cozy, nostalgic feel. It is finished with "mud paint", an old Swedish covering for exterior wood. The classic color is reddish-brown, but it is available in a whole range of colors: yellow (yellow ocher), black, brown (umbra), white, blue, or green. The oldest and most widely used pigment is Swedish red, a byproduct of copper mining at Stora Kopparberg, near the town of Falun in Dalarna, central Sweden.

▶ The common cowslip (*Primula veris*) grows wild in several places in southern Sweden, including in the hills of Brösarp, also called the gateway to Österlen.

A Beautiful Garden in Southern Sweden

▲ I sat at this table with Kerstin and friends in late August 2019, enjoying coffee after lunch. That warm and sunny afternoon was the last time we gathered in her beautiful garden. It's great to know that the garden is in good hands. Kerstin's daughters have been coming here since they were little, when it belonged to their grandparents. There is something very special about houses and gardens being handed down through the same family for several generations.

▶ The house still bears some traces from its days as a fisherman's cottage without running water. The pump still works. When I was last there, Kerstin was still using it regularly. It is becoming quite fashionable to reinstall these cast-iron pumps on top of rainwater tanks.

▶ The apple trees bloom merrily in Kerstin's garden, just as they do in the countryside around Kivik, which is dotted with orchards as far as the eye can see. The hills facing the Baltic Sea have an ideal climate for growing apples, so this area is also known as Sweden's apple kingdom. Around two-thirds of all apples consumed in Sweden are produced in an area the size of a thousand soccer fields Driving through the countryside in mid-May, when the low, crooked trees are shrouded in pink blossoms, is a great experience. Not to mention late summer, when red, yellow, and green apples bring color to the landscape. A truly breathtaking sight!

▼ A visit to Kiviks Musteri is highly recommended. An entire industry has grown up here around apple products, and Swedes and Danes make pilgrimages here to fill both their cars and their bellies. Next door is Äpplets Hus, where you can learn about different apple varieties, get advice on growing your own apples, and follow the fruit's path through to end products.

▲ Kerstin's garden has plenty of seating, and as a welcoming and gracious host, she used them regularly. She always had time to chat. She was a good listener, with a broad range of interests. We didn't just talk about gardens but also about other important things in life, like art and culture.

◀ Kerstin was an expert in the kitchen and spoiled her guests, but she wasn't much for kitchen gardens, making do with just a few herbs and some chives.

228   The Cottage Garden

▲ Kerstin was always on the go, forever embarking on new plans and projects. For example, she laid the paving in this square in front of the house. Every single stone was chosen with care. She would often walk along the seafront and come home with full pockets. The different-sized tiles were already there.

▲ Walking around Kivik in midsummer is intoxicating. Rarely have I been anywhere with as many roses as here. The mild coastal climate clearly suits them. Old records, photos, and paintings show that they have been part of Österlen for centuries.

◀ Sweet William (*Dianthus barbatus*) also loves it here. Elsewhere, it is usually an annual that withers and dies in the fall. But here, it returns year after year and even self-seeds in cracks and crevices.

▲ There's something classic about red roses. When you see them against the white fence, it's hard to imagine a more perfect pairing. Pastel shades are lovely, of course, but sometimes you need something bolder. The rose is called 'Hansaland'. It is a very hardy and richly flowering variety from the German breeder Kordes.

▶ The passion for roses here is so great that a dedicated association, Österlen Roses, was set up to share information and knowledge about the town's cultural and historical connection to these wonderful flowers. For several decades, the association has been registering heirloom varieties in Österlen. So far, over two hundred varieties have been documented and described in text and pictures on its website.

◀ Kerstin's grandmother and grandfather lived near Helsingborg, and she had many fond memories of their garden. She—like her grandmother before her—loved the rose 'New Dawn'. It was introduced in 1930 by the Somerset Rose Nursery in New Jersey. 'New Dawn' was voted the most popular rose at the 1997 World Convention of Rose Societies. It is so beloved because of its charming, semi-double pink flowers and incredible lushness.

A Beautiful Garden in Southern Sweden   231

◀ Kerstin spent many years pruning the boxwood. She started off small by planting cuttings but had no real plans for them. The shapes emerged along the way and today create a uniquely cozy atmosphere while also adding stature and a focal point—especially in the winter garden. Boxwood remains green all year round.

▲ Kerstin always had a soft spot for red roses, especially 'Flammentanz'. While the individual flowers are highly appealing, the growth on this shrub, with its drooping, bare "leggy" stem, leaves something to be desired. Still, it looks graceful up against the old house. 'Flammentanz' can reach up to 13 to 16 feet (4 to 5 m). The flowers have a pleasant fragrance. Unfortunately, it only flowers once a season, so enjoy them while they last.

▲ 'Gerbe Rose' is an heirloom variety with beautiful pink flowers that has a scent similar to that of peonies. Kerstin bought this variety from the rose nursery Roskraft in Borrby, about 19 miles (30 km) south of Kivik. Roskraft is a small nursery with a very large selection—around one thousand different species and varieties. What's special about this particular nursery is that its roses are rooted and grown from cuttings, just like in the old days. Today, the vast majority of garden roses are grafted onto a wild stem, as it's more economical. At Roskraft, however, they believe that the old-fashioned methods produce better roses.

◀ ▲ 'Super Dorothy' is another of the garden's many climbing roses. It can grow up to about 13 feet tall (about 4 m) and is unusually flower rich. The small pink flowers sit in clusters and spring out every few days. They have a pleasant but not very strong scent. In the picture above, 'Super Dorothy' is intertwined with 'Gerbe Rose'! It grows into the small tree as the long shoots reach down toward the ground.

A Beautiful Garden in Southern Sweden

A Beautiful Garden in Southern Sweden

▲ This photograph, at first glance, may seem to depict a giant rose bush, like the one in P. S. Krøyer's (1851–1909) painting *Garden Party with Marie Krøyer and Roses* from 1893, only even bigger! But no, it's the climbing rose 'François Juranville', which has sent its shoots up into an old apple tree. It's an absolutely amazing sight! The shoots of this beautiful climbing rose can be up to 20 to 23 feet (6 to 7 m) long, so this is a perfect way to plant it. Grow it up a trellis, and 'François Juranville' will really take off. 'François Juranville' received one of the greatest accolades in the plant world, the Award of Garden Merit from the Royal Horticultural Society (RHS). Since 1922, this stamp of quality has been awarded to summer flowers, perennials, shrubs, and trees that have passed the RHS's rigorous testing program in Wisley Garden, Surrey, England.

▶ Another rose growing upward into one of the garden's many fruit trees. This one is 'Super Excelsa', one of the smaller climbing roses, which grows to a couple of yards (meters) tall.

▶ 'Princess Alexandra Renaissance' is a Danish-bred rose from the well-known company Poulsen Roser, which has been in existence for nearly 150 years. There are quite a few Renaissance roses, including the famous 'Ghita Renaissance', named after the Danish actor Ghita Nørby. Renaissance roses are hybrids of heirloom and modern roses, with double flowers, a classic look, and a lovely scent. They are robust, hardy, and healthy and bloom throughout the season.

▼ The long stems of 'François Juranville' hang like garlands over a small seat.

▲ It has always amazed me that there are relatively few white- to cream-colored climbing roses, at least among the large-flowered types. There are some slightly more "wild" varieties with small flowers and long shoots in the style of 'François Juranville' (see pages 234–236). If you're looking for a climbing rose that won't grow too wildly and has relatively large, cream-white flowers, 'Ilse Krohn Superior' is a good choice.

▶ 'Ilse Krohn Superior' has creamy white flowers, up to 4 inches (10 cm) across with distinctive curly petals. This is a healthy and very hardy rose with a lovely scent. It seems to have been somewhat forgotten and deserves to be dusted off.

▶ 'Paul's Himalayan Musk' was introduced in the nineteenth century but not registered until 1915. The small, full, white-pink flowers spring out in early June and have a truly addictive, captivating scent. It takes three or four years to reach its full height—around 4 to 5 yards (4 to 5 m). Here it is seen using a tree as a host plant.

▼ When it comes to photographing roses, the biggest challenge is timing. Luckily, things worked out nicely in Kerstin's garden. Among other things, the impressive 'Paul's Himalayan Musk' was at its best when I visited on June 20, just before midsummer.

▼ The giant bellflower (*Campanula latifolia*) is an easy and beautiful perennial that grows to well over 3 feet (1 m) tall. Like all other bellflowers, it has a slightly wild look that makes it a perfect addition to a cottage garden.

A Special Harmony

I am so grateful that I was invited to visit and photograph South Wood Farm in Dorset. This is a special place with a lovely, harmonious feel. I had seen it in several English gardening magazines and was always fascinated by the soul and charm it exudes.

The buildings here date back to the 1400s. For centuries, this was a farm with dairy cattle. In 1993, the herd was sold, and the farm changed hands. The new owners lived here until 2005, when a couple from London bought the house to use as a vacation home. The couple was entranced by the buildings and surrounding landscape—there was no garden to speak of at that time.

They contacted garden and landscape architect Arne Maynard, one of England's most highly respected designers—especially when it comes to the grounds around historic buildings. Arne's work—not only with plants but also with wood, stone, and iron—is truly enchanting. He adopts a holistic approach to design and always incorporates the surrounding landscape and its history, as well as the buildings themselves, and of course, the wishes of his clients. In his work, architecture, garden history, and long-forgotten traditional crafts and techniques go hand in hand.

His style is very British and might be described as discreet and understated.

One of Arne's great strengths is his ability to bring in exactly the right people. Not just the many and versatile artists in his design studio but also artisans and gardeners. The head gardeners tasked with realizing his designs are often people he has trained himself, and they are in a league of their own.

One of them is Will Smithson, an Instagram acquaintance who helped me secure an invitation to South Wood Farm. Will is incredibly passionate, and it's obvious how much he admires Arne and his team. He told me how the

different gardeners from Arne's gardens regularly meet to share tips and inspire each other.

Will left South Wood Farm after seven years. He moved to Tuscany with his wife and children, where he is the head gardener at La Petraia, a relatively new garden designed by Arne.

I look forward to following Will's new adventure on Instagram: @solegardener

A Special Harmony   241

▲ A narrow path passes through wild vegetation to reach the house. It looks like these paths and trees have always been there—which was the idea, of course—but everything has actually been redesigned. The parking area has been moved so that it is out of sight, and new paths have been laid. Espalier-trained pear trees mark the transition from the wild meadow to the slightly more cultivated gravel garden.

▶ The trimmed shrubs and trees make for a highly effective contrast to the wild, natural areas. Notice how the grass is cut to form paths.

▲ ▶ Just before the stairs to the courtyard in front of the house is a small gravel garden. Drought-tolerant plants are allowed to self-seed here. The trick is to make everything look a bit spontaneous, but not too much— a delicate balance that the English are particularly good at striking. Nothing has been left to chance. Selective weeding prevents it from looking *too* wild. Good plants for gravel gardens include daisy (*Leucanthemum vulgare*), Macedonian scabious (*Knautia macedonica*), foxglove (*Digitalis*), mullein (*Verbascum*), red valerian (*Centranthus ruber*), and purple top (*Verbena bonariensis*).

A Special Harmony   243

▲ Arne Maynard uses oak for doors, columns, and garden furniture. This is a durable hardwood with a long life that ages gracefully, turning grayish with time. Another significant factor is that oak is an indigenous British tree, which has been used for house-building and half-timbering for centuries.

► The courtyard has a nice, tight design with a central gravel path that divides the space diagonally around a central, topiaried laurel tree, *Laurus nobilis*. Thyme grows in the diamond-shaped bed under the tree.

▲ Catmint (*Nepeta faassenii*), 'Walker's Low', is a slightly wild growth that nicely complements the old stone pot. On the wall is a rose trellis made of hazelnut branches.

▶ The floral hues include white, pink, and blue, complemented by abundant green foliage. Various alliums bloom alongside the dark lupin 'Masterpiece'. At the front, the lilac sage (*Salvia verticillata*) 'Purple Rain' is on its way.

▼ The entrance to the house is offset from the center and accessible via a tiled walkway flanked by box-shaped yew bushes. Each "box" consists of sixteen plants. Lavender has been planted between the tightly cut yews.

▶ Hazel cuttings are used to support the perennials. In the early spring, Will sticks the branches in the ground between perennials that he knows are likely to topple over. It's all a matter of timing, and the good thing is that the hazel is invisible once the perennials grow. In this case, the perennials are asters.

▲ Here, three sections of lawn interact with the other green plants. The boundaries of the gravel paths are made of strips of steel welded together at right angles. The metal borders mean that the edges of the lawn do not have to be constantly re-cut.

◀ The double-flowered cranesbill (*Geranium pratense*) 'Summer Skies' has lavender-blue flowers resembling small roses. It flowers well and easily.

▼ Between the lawn sections and the beds are narrow paths made of hard-fired bricks, which nicely delineate the layout. The reinforced steel strips are clearly visible here too.

◀ This may not have been the first great masterwort (*Astrantia major*), but it is certainly one of the best. Called 'Roma', its beautiful pink flowers make it a hit in bouquets. Feel free to pluck them to your heart's content, because even if all the flowering stems are removed, a second wave will arrive in late summer.

▲ Many of the trimmed shrubs seen in the garden, including this "plug," are yew. The same goes for the layers in the picture at the top of the previous page. Topiary is the art of shaping trees and shrubs. This is a discipline that has its origins all the way back to ancient Rome, although its heyday was in Renaissance and Baroque gardens, when parterre beds were considered highly fashionable by the aristocracy. Later, topiary made its way into farmer's and cottage gardens—first in the form of low boxwood hedges and later artfully cut figures such as birds. This is a painstaking, time-consuming art, but the living sculptures, especially larger figures, give a garden a classic feel.

▶ One particularly special allium is this purple *Allium atropurpureum*, which has the darkest flowers in this group. It's not one of the easiest alliums to grow—at least not in my garden. Perhaps my soil is too clay-rich and moist, although that doesn't seem to be a problem for other alliums, which return year after year.

A Special Harmony   247

◄ ▲ When you open the gate and climb a few steps, a completely new experience awaits—the kitchen garden, which is in a class of its own. I will return to it soon. Arne Maynard likes to work with levels, as he enjoys the varied effects produced by changes in terrain. He also likes to use gates and doors, which make you curious to see what is hidden on the other side.

▲ In terms of topiary, two main species are used here. First is yew, which is used for both the "boxes" in the foreground and the "plug" in the middle of the photo. Boxwood used to be common, but its popularity has declined somewhat, as it is highly vulnerable to fungal attacks. In the last twenty years, many boxwood plants have died.

In the middle is a bay tree, *Laurus nobilis*. This particular type is not often seen in England but is found all over the Mediterranean.

In England, holly is also often cut into shapes. Privet and *Thuja* are other options, and beech and hornbeam are also worth a mention. The latter, in particular, can be cut very tightly. Especially in the Netherlands and Belgium, it is used for box- and umbrella-shaped trees, columns, and, of course, hedges. In Denmark, however, the common beech is the tree most frequently used for topiary. The advantage is that beech retains its foliage in the winter, while hornbeam sheds it in the fall.

◀ Meadow cranesbill (*Geranium pratense*) is another easy and graceful perennial that thrives in both sun and partial shade.

A Special Harmony 249

▲ The English seem to be particularly good at establishing, maintaining, and caring for flower meadows. This is an extremely interesting topic. Given our current interest in biodiversity, I believe and hope that we will see even more meadows in the future.

◀ To encourage flowering and prevent the grass from suffocating the bloom, you have to starve the soil. See page 61 for details of how Michael Chalupka does it.

In England, I learned if you want to establish a flower meadow, one particular plant is essential: yellow rattle (*Rhinanthus minor*). The reason for this is that the 4- to 8-inch-tall (10- to 20-cm) plant is semi-parasitic, with both taproots and side roots. The roots attach themselves to a suitable species (often a grass) and then extract water and minerals until the host dies.

To germinate, these seeds need a prolonged cold period, so it's important to sow between August and January. If you are in the process of planting a flower meadow on a bare piece of land, yellow rattle seeds can be mixed with the others before sowing.

As a counterpoint to the wild flowering meadow, the kitchen garden is surrounded by a traditional English lawn. While I don't have grass in my garden, I am curious to learn how you go about creating such a beautiful lawn. Will offers some tips.

First, fork the lawn, wiggling the tool back and forth. Then use a scarifier to remove moss. Use the highest-quality grass seeds—the lawn must contain a minimum of four different species and varieties. This helps the grass develop into a neat and uniform lawn, even though the growing conditions will not be the same everywhere. Some species thrive in the shade, while others need full sun. To even out bumps, add a thin layer of sand —not more than 0.2 inch (5 mm). Fertilize the lawn three times—in April, May/June, and August/September.

Lawns became especially popular with the aristocracy of northwestern Europe during the Renaissance. Before the invention of the lawnmower in 1830, only the wealthy could afford to hire enough staff to maintain them. Different maintenance methods were used, but all of them were very labor-intensive, especially in large areas. Grass was kept at bay with, for example, a scythe, sickle, or sheep shears. Sheep, cattle, or deer were often used as four-legged lawnmowers.

▶ The beautiful fruit cages that keep the birds out are a trademark feature of Arne Maynard's gardens.

The kitchen garden is used to grow
not only vegetables but also flowers
for bouquets. Sweet peas are a regular
part of the cycle and are precultivated
in the greenhouse so they flower
as early as possible. Later, another
batch is sown outdoors to prolong
the season.

Seasonal vegetables are harvested
and prepared in the kitchen. And there
are always fresh flowers on the table
when the owners come for weekends.

The owners often entertain guests, and Will takes pride in the fact that the garden supplies vegetables all year round. Cabbage is a very important crop—but as we know, its existence is fairly precarious, as it will almost certainly be attacked by larvae between June and late summer.

To stop the white cabbage butterfly from laying eggs on the leaves, nets protect the plants starting in early spring. But make sure that they don't touch the cabbage leaves, because then you run the risk of butterflies being able to lay eggs through the net.

▲ In many gardens, a greenhouse is absolutely essential, and South Wood Farm is no exception. Many plants—both flowers and vegetables—are grown in it first and then moved out into the garden. Will says that the busiest period starts in February. For the next couple of months, the greenhouse is packed with plants. In April, assuming it's not too cold, they start planting out in the garden.

◀ ▶ The greenhouse isn't insulated but has modern conveniences such as thermostatically controlled heating mats that prevent the plants from getting cold feet. The mats are necessary when sowing or propagating cuttings in early spring.

▲ The greenhouse is partially sunken and stands in the center of the kitchen garden. The beautiful wooden frame comes from the English company WG Grace & Son, which has been making wooden greenhouses for the past thirty years. Today, the company uses Accoya, a type of treated Nordic pine. The treatment process is called acetylation and turns the otherwise quite soft pine into a hard, stable, and weather-resistant material, which helps significantly extend its service life. The manufacturer guarantees a lifespan of fifty years outdoors.

The wood is treated with acetic anhydride at 212°F to 248°F (100 to 120°C). The acetic acid binds to the hydroxyl groups in the wood and blocks the absorption of moisture while increasing the density of the wood by about 8 percent. The increased density means that the wood can't absorb water, so it's not susceptible to fungus or rot.

▲ Most alliums are purple, but there are also white ones. One particularly pretty species is black garlic (*Allium nigrum*), with distinctive, hemispherical flowers. Notice the cold frames (previously seen on page 252 and page 258).

◀ ▶ Hazel is used everywhere—as supports for plants and even in Will's scarecrow. If hazel is planted in the sun, the stem will be slightly crooked, but new shoots from the base or roots will be long and straight.

▶ It is really important to support plants *before* they fall over. There are many types of racks and frames on the market, but everything at South Wood Farm is homemade. This pleasing arrangement of hazel branches is stapled together.

▲ In the past, cottage gardens made use of local, readily available materials. They simply had no other choice. It was about making something out of nothing. Here, hazel is used to support various pea plants that will soon form a green hedge.

◄ Chives (*Allium schoenoprasum*) are indispensable in the kitchen and also beautiful in the garden when in bloom. This is a perennial that can be propagated either from seed or by dividing. When sowing seeds, remember that they will not flower until the second year.

▲ Hazelnut branches, sticks, and twigs are harvested from shrubs planted as hedgerows many years ago. Lopping shears are used to cut off the thickest branches right at the base, which allows new ones to emerge. This use of hazel was Arne Maynard's idea, and he makes sure that all of his gardeners learn this skill. Hopefully, other gardeners will be inspired to do so too. The great thing is that you can prepare these supports in the preseason, when there's not much to do in the garden.

▲ True craftsmanship shines through everywhere, not least in the beautiful oak raised beds.

◄ A small stock of plants stands by, ready to be planted once the soil is bare. Most are made on site and propagated from seeds or cuttings.

▲ The yard has been lovingly restored, and many of the stones have been reused. In several places, the walls have been renovated and rebuilt. There are a great many English craftspeople who have mastered old techniques. Further, it is possible to get ahold of recycled materials and architectural features—a number of companies specialize in this. Aged, almost dilapidated garden furniture also has a role to play.

▶ Old stone troughs are incredibly popular and help to create a timeless, authentic feel. It is all about conveying a sense of history. Aged, almost dilapidated garden furniture is also part of the narrative.

▲ When the owners first saw this place, they fell in love with the unspoiled setting—which was very authentic but not in great condition. Although it has been vastly improved, nothing has been modernized.

One of the reasons Arne was chosen for the task was that, in addition to being a formidable garden and landscape designer, he has a profound understanding of building and construction. It was important to draw up an overall plan for this place, and he did so in consultation with both his design studio staff and outside experts. The job is not yet finished—according to Will's Instagram account, a parterre garden has just been completed.

▼ The old coach house was cleared and now offers seating where visitors can shelter from the sun or rain.

► This small daisy-like growth, Mexican fleabane (*Erigeron karvinskianus*), is found all over England. It self-seeds in brickwork and between stones—in fact, just about anywhere—and is a perennial that survives mild winters.

A Special Harmony 265

Arne Maynard also suggested building a sun parlor—not just for use by the owners but also as a space where Will and his team could take breaks. Half of the wall and the roof of the old building next to the coach house were removed and replaced with glass panels. This is a beautiful solution that required only minimal disruption. Arne designed both the glass house and the external plant theater.

JOBS JUNE

STAKE FC

PLANT OUT DAHLIAS

PLANT OUT MORE PEAS & BEETS

PLANT UP POTS & TROUGHS

WEED STREAM & AROUND POND

HAVE FIRE

PRUNE PLUMS

The solid tables are also by Arne. He partners with carpenters to design and produce furniture for many of his gardens.

The German term *Gesamtkunstwerk* (artistic synthesis or total work of art), coined by the philosopher Karl Friedrich Eusebius Trahndorff (1782–1863), perfectly encapsulates Arne's approach.

Follow Arne Maynard at @arnemaynardgardendesign.

A Special Harmony 267

Pure Cottage Style

When my interest in gardens started more than twenty-five years ago, England was my first love. For many years, I would head to the UL in search of inspiration. Later, my attention turned to France, specifically Normandy, and later again to the Netherlands, Belgium, Sweden, and the United States. However, for some reason, I barely know Germany at all—which is a bit odd given how close it is to my home.

In 2018, I decided that the time had come to explore the neighboring country's gardens. Turning to Instagram, I found a number of beautiful gardens south of the Danish border and set off in mid-July. The goal was to travel as far south as Munich. I was full of anticipation.

I had done my homework and made contact with several gardeners I wanted to visit. I had found some via social media, others by word of mouth. After all, not all garden owners are on social media—such as the owners of Ibba Garten, which is next up.

During my trips, I often ask online followers to recommend gardens along my route. That's exactly how I heard about Ibba Garten, which I then searched for on Google. I could only find a few pictures but was taken by it right away. This place—both the house and the garden—exuded pure cottage style. I simply had to visit it! It was virtually impossible to find contact information, but in the end, I did manage to get in touch with the owners, Hilde and Raymund Ibba. After hearing about my trip, they invited me to visit them in Höfen, North Rhine-Westphalia, a couple of hundred miles southwest of Cologne, very close to both the Belgian and Dutch borders.

Hilde and Raymund turned out to be extremely likeable, and visiting them at the end of July was a delightful experience. Both the garden and the house (which dates from 1658) were in a class of their own. The couple moved here in 1979 to provide a good life for their six children, all born on the farm.

Back then, the place wasn't the paradise it is today. The house really needed some love and attention. There used to be farm animals here, but Raymund turned the stables into housing.

There was no garden, just an adjoining plot of land measuring approximately 1.5 acres (6,000 sq m) where cows had been kept. A neighbor plowed it for them, and they planted potatoes to get the soil going. The following year, Hilde began planting a kitchen garden measuring about 700 square yards (600 sq m), followed by a flower garden, which now covers an impressive half an acre (2,000 sq m).

Ibba Garten was a great place to visit, and I really fancied following it over a whole season, so we agreed that I would return in April 2019. In fact, I drove the 1,000-mile (1,700-km) round trip no less than five times last year.

As well as being a great pleasure to visit a garden several times, it is also highly instructive and means that the book shows how much things change in the course of a year.

Not that you can tell from the pictures, but on the morning of April 10, the ground was white with snow. I had arrived the night before and was astonished to wake up and see that it had been snowing—and still was—not a thick layer but enough to cover the ground.

On the way down through Germany, it had been nice spring weather, but Hilde and Raymund had prepared me for life in a relatively cold area. Höfen is in the Eifel Mountains, the highest point of which is almost 2,500 feet (750 m) above sea level.

Luckily, the snow melted during the day, so the photoshoot could go ahead. Everything was ready for the new season, and plants had already been sown under covers.

Every time I visit Hilde and Raymund, I stay in picturesque Monschau, just a few miles from Höfen, which is full of the most beautiful half-timbered houses. One of the fringe benefits of traveling to so many gardens is that you get to visit places you would otherwise never see.

Monschau's history can be traced back to the Middle Ages, but in the seventeenth and eighteenth centuries, it flourished as a center of textile production. The river Roer, which runs through the town, provided hydropower to the textile mills. Many of the listed buildings in the area date from this period.

The Belgian border is within walking distance from the town.

Pure Cottage Style   271

▲ The good thing about visiting the garden in April is that at this time of year, both the kitchen and the flower garden are a hive of activity. In some places, wire mesh is in place for the plants to climb. Later in the season, this archway will be completely covered by the common hop (*Humulus lupulus*) 'Aureus', which dies back every winter before returning in spring.

▶ There is something so rich with potential about a plot of land that has been prepared for cultivation. But it doesn't take long before most of the garden is covered with beautiful crops— both vegetables and flowers.

▲ During spring, the fields around the garden resound with life—and lots of bleating, as the newly born lambs demand milk. Raymund and the couple's sons look after the sheep.

The breed, Coburger Fuchsschaf, is an old one found only in a few places in Germany. One of its distinctive characteristics is that the lambs are reddish-brown at birth. The color fades as they grow, but even the adult sheep sometimes have a slight reddish tinge.

Hilde used to spin the wool herself, but these days she sends it to the company Das Goldene Vlies for processing.

▶ Hilde is a rose lover, especially old heirloom ones, and the garden features over two hundred different varieties. Some of them grow rapidly and require support. This wooden tower blends in well with its surroundings.

▶ Hilde strives to make the garden attractive to local wildlife by planting bee-friendly flowers. This has become fashionable in recent years, but for Hilde it is no novelty.

◀ ▲ Hilde and Raymund put a huge amount of effort into producing their own compost—large quantities every year. The garden is based on biodynamic principles, and compost is an important source of nutrition. The recipe includes old straw, which is used for bedding for the sheep, but also kitchen waste such as potato peelings, egg and nut shells, coffee grounds, and tea leaves—and even paper towels and egg cartons. Finally, of course, it involves garden waste such as perennial tops, grass clippings, branches, leaves, cabbage stumps, lettuce leftovers, and fallen fruit. Everything is finely chopped to speed up the process.

The ingredients are stacked in long troughs—alternating layers of animal bedding and kitchen and garden waste—and then covered with tarpaulin. The compost is regularly stirred and turned over. In spring, it is sieved, and then it is ready to be spread in the garden beds, giving the new plants a massive nutritional boost.

▶ Wire fencing is used to divide spaces. The consistent use of rusty iron gives the garden a coherent feel. The good thing about wire is that it doesn't draw too much attention to itself. In the flower garden, it is used to support roses.

▲ When you bend long rose stalks, as seen here, many more flowers will bud. All the leaf axils burst open into flower-bearing shoots. This makes the flowering much more sumptuous (see the picture on page 298).

▶ There are different types of peony. In early spring, when the plants start to shoot, the leaves on the garden peony are gathered at the top of the stem, as in the picture, while in other types they are more spread out. The common peony, *Paeonia officinalis*, is a southern European species that blooms in the second half of May, a few weeks before the ordinary peony (also called silk peony). The common peony is not quite as tall and almost always has double carmine-red flowers. *Paeonia lactiflora* comes from China and is available in a variety of colors and shapes, both single- and double-flowering.

▲ The flower garden is next to the kitchen garden and is about three times as big. Hilde grows many plants in the small greenhouse (which features a wood-burning stove) as well as in the brick chimney and polytunnel. Being located up in the mountains, the garden is quite cool, especially in spring, so it's good to have a head start before moving the plants out into the garden.

▶ Broad-leaved grape hyacinth (*Muscari latifolium*) differs slightly from the well-known species Armenian grape hyacinth (*Muscari armeniacum*), which has solid-colored flowers. As seen here, the former's inflorescences are dark at the bottom and light at the top, producing a stunning effect.

▼ *Primula vulgaris*, the common primrose, lights up the spring garden.

► Two pieces of wire fencing join at the top form an arch. It doesn't get much simpler. It is vital that the rose doesn't grow so much that the whole thing collapses. The common cowslip (*Primula veris*) thrives in the garden and self-seeds in convenient spots.

▲ There's no spring without daffodils. One of the remarkable things about the Eifel Mountains are the wild daffodils (*Narcissus pseudonarcissus*). Large numbers grow around Monschau, attracting hikers and nature-loving tourists from Germany and the surrounding countries.

▶ The spring flowering lasts quite a long time in the cool mountain landscape. Fortunately, the daffodils cope well with occasional temperature dips. However, if extreme cold is in the forecast, Hilde covers the ground with sprigs of spruce—and in the case of the kitchen garden, fabric.

▲ The lenten rose (*Helleborus orientalis*), also grows well here. It is rare to see these in such large groups. This beautiful plant self-seeds willingly. When the seedlings are a couple of years old, Hilde replants them elsewhere in the garden and pampers them with fresh compost. The problem with seedlings is that they often grow right on top of each other around the mother plant. If you don't thin them out, they will simply suffocate each other. The lenten rose usually flowers for the first time a couple of years after being moved, so it's a bit of a slow starter.

▶ A quickly assembled support made of sticks for a newly planted rose. Once it starts to grow rapidly, it will need more support.

◀ Horn violet (*Viola cornuta*) is one of the easiest spring plants. As it dies back, it sends out seeds that will bloom the following spring. It's always exciting to see how the flowers turn out, because you're never sure what you'll get. The different plants crossbreed with each other, resulting in beautiful color variations. But I have yet to find a variety I don't like.

▲ Looking at the sparse, slightly bare April garden, it's hard to imagine that in just a couple of months, the ground will be completely covered. Stepping stones are an excellent idea to avoid trampling down the soil.

◀ Few plants have such small, delicate, and fragrant flowers as the sweet violet (*Viola odorata*). It is incredible that such a small flower has such a strong and lovely scent. During the growing season, the decorative, rounded leaves grow substantially and form dense ground cover, interacting beautifully with other leafy plants.

▼ The garden has a lot of raised bird boxes on poles. When I asked about the upturned-bowl-like arrangement under the box, Hilde explained that it stops cats from climbing up.

▼ A peek in the greenhouse, where the herbs are ready to be planted in the kitchen garden.

Pure Cottage Style   281

Three weeks later, I am back for my second visit. It is now May 4, and the kitchen garden is starting to look crowded.

The kitchen garden is Hilde's great passion, and the family is fully self-sufficient in food. The soil is cultivated biodynamically according to the principles of anthroposophy developed by the Austrian philosopher Rudolf Steiner (1861–1925). According to Steiner, the entire universe is governed not only by known physical forces but also by cosmic ones. These forces affect the life processes of plants, animals, and humans. Biodynamics consciously seeks to work with these forces by finding methods of horticulture and agriculture that approach nature as a harmonious, living organism.

In many ways, Germany is a pioneer in health and wellness, and biodynamic thinking started there in 1924.

▲ Notice how Hilde lays out long boards to avoid trampling down the earth.

▶ ▶ The golden hop (*Humulus lupulus*) 'Aureus' begins to shoot in early May and grows fast. You can almost see it growing day by day. In a few months, it will cover the entire tunnel. The decorative lime-yellow tone of the foliage is most pronounced at the beginning of the season. As the weeks go by, the leaves gradually become greener.

▲ The beautiful farmhouse, which is more than three hundred years old, is one of the oldest buildings in the village. Looking after such a place is a lifestyle in itself. Luckily, Raymund is a great craftsman who likes to use his hands. He has also passed on his skills to the next generation. When I first visited the family, the four men— with help from the women—were replacing the thatched roof.

▶ There are a few tulips in the garden, and every year, Hilde plants new bulbs. The problem is that water voles, of which there are a few here, love the bulbs, which makes life hard for the tulips. Daffodils fare better because voles don't like them.

▶ The area around Monschau is characterized by remarkably high hedges, planted to protect against the strong mountain winds. I've never seen such impressive hedges. There's no doubt that they are effective. The hedges are up to 23 to 26 feet (7 to 8 m) high, and it is said that some were planted back in the seventeenth and eighteenth centuries. There are around five hundred of them in the area. In some places, they enclose entire sites. On the main road between Höfen and Monschau, glimpsed through an opening in the fortress-like hedge, is a half-timbered house. It must be the most photographed home for miles around.

My third visit was on June 8. The roses in my own garden were in full blossom. But not in Höfen, Hilde had warned me. I had a hard time believing that, because the further south I drove, the more the roses were in bloom.

But when I arrived at the foot of the mountains and started to make my way upwards, I could see that she was right. The roses there hadn't started to bloom yet.

Pure Cottage Style   285

▲ In the kitchen garden, much had changed in the three weeks since my last visit, but the danger of night frost still loomed. Hilde told me she had covered the crops with cloth several times in recent weeks and fired up the wood-burning stove in the little greenhouse. Fortunately, nothing died, and the forecast for the next week was warm.

▲ A glorious sight. Notice the huge green garden angelica (*Angelica archangelica*) on the left. This was one of the first plants to be grown in Denmark, where the Vikings set up what are referred to as "monastic" gardens. Angelica was used in cooking and medicine. The thick root contains essential oils, organic acids, and tannins, and was used to treat kidney problems, abdominal pain, and toothache.

◄ It was a pleasant surprise to see the bearded German iris (*Iris germanica*) mix so beautifully with other flowers, because it is rather fond of heat.

Pure Cottage Style   287

▲ Rows of chives. Notice also the *Angelica archangelica*, as described on the previous page. Its growth here really is impressive. Angelica is a biennial, so it dies after flowering.

▶ The golden hops mentioned earlier have almost reached the top of the arch. The lime-yellow color of the leaf allows it to be seen from a distance. Later in the season, it turns green. Before the summer is over, the hops will cover the entire archway before dying back in the fall.

◀ This pink wild perennial (*Silene viscaria*), the 'Sticky Catchfly', has stems that are sticky, as if smeared in sap. "Wild perennial" means that the plant is found in the wild. This one particularly likes dry places.

▼ Celeriac and various cabbages have been planted in the kitchen garden. They start off life in the greenhouse to give them a head start.

▲ A lot has happened since I was last here. Compare this with the large photo on page 284—there's no bare ground left. Everything looks so lush and full of promise. The garden roses that line the arches and racks are bedecked in thousands of buds. It's important to enjoy the moment, of course, but it's also hard to be patient when you're waiting for all these magnificent roses to bloom.

◄ The bright yellow flowers are Welsh poppies (*Meconopsis cambrica*), which brighten up many corners of the garden. They are straightforward to grow and also thrive in the shade.

▶ Greater meadow rue (*Thalictrum aquilegifolium*) is the earliest flowering of its species.

▶ There is something very special about wild flowers such as thistles. The problem is that in a garden setting, they may get just a little too wild because they self-seed. This is not a problem with this perennial plume thistle (*Cirsium rivulare*) 'Atropurpureum', which is sterile and doesn't produce seeds. It looks so beautiful here in a large group.

▼ Jacob's ladder (*Polemonium caeruleum*) is also a perennial—albeit a short-lived one. This is a mountain plant often seen in Norway and Sweden. The slightly peculiar name alludes to the foliage, which resembles several small ladders. Jacob's ladder is often blue but sometimes white.

▼ When I return
in early July, the
cabbages and herbs
are growing well.

◀ Variegated
horseradish (*Armoracia
rusticana*) 'Variegata'
is not seen very often.
Some might call the
leaf impressive rather
than pretty, but it
will look adorable in a
white bed. However, be
aware that horseradish
spreads rapidly—you
might want to try it
in a pot first.

▲ The kitchen garden is a wonderful mix of flowers, vegetables, berries, and fruit. There are also beautiful red poppies here and there. Hilda often picks them for bouquets. When the children are at home, they like to get busy with the shears. There are plenty of vegetables, thanks not only to Hilde and Raymund but also to the younger generations who occasionally lend a helping hand.

▶ Borage or starflower (*Borago officinalis*). These star-shaped flowers, standing tall and swaying gently in the breeze, are notable for their hairy leaves, stems, and buds. I saw them growing in the wild in many places when I was in Finland several years ago. They also come in white.

◀ The beetroots are also well on their way. Hilde uses the young leaves in salads.

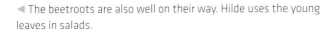

▲ Wire fencing space dividers stop the plants spreading out onto the grass. They also give the garden structure, which can be important when working with beds as lush as these.

◀ Umbel-flowered catchfly (*Silene orientalis*) is another wild plant. On the whole, Hilde has a penchant for wild species—i.e., ones not cultivated by breeders. This makes sense here in the cold mountain climate, where more refined varieties can struggle to survive.

▼ The roses are not in full bloom until early July. This is the very best time to visit. Hilde has several hundred roses arrayed over fences, columns, and arches. This is the lush pink rose 'Dentelle de Bruxelles'. The somewhat shorter white rose is 'Hedi Grimm'.

▲ Kohlrabi gradually develops a round stem node a few inches above the ground. This is a highly decorative vegetable, also found in violet. The edible part is the round "knot," which is at its most delicious when it's the size of a small apple. If allowed to grow larger, it becomes somewhat woody.

▼ Cornflower needs some form of support to ensure it doesn't tip over.

Pure Cottage Style   295

◄ 'Blush Damask' is an adorable rose that needs a little elbow room because it tends to spread out. It also has some overhanging growth, so the area by the chestnut fence is a good spot for it.

▲ 'Blauwschokker' is a highly decorative pea with really dark pods. They grow to around 6 feet tall (2 m). The young peas can be eaten as mangetout, along with the pods, and used as a garnish in a salad. But if you let the peas develop, discard the pods. The blue flowers and the top shoots both work well in a salad.

▲ ▶ I always learn something new when I visit other people's gardens. For example, Hilde mentioned a delicious type of strawberry called Himbeererdbeere (raspberry strawberries). This is an old species bred in eastern Germany in 1925 by Otto Schindler. They are also called framberries and strasberries in English.

These quite small berries are delicate, round, and deep red. As the name suggests, they taste like a combination of raspberries and strawberries. They are super-sweet and highly delicious, and fantastic for pickling. Hilde grows the variety 'Mieze Schindler' and also 'Schindler Nova', which was bred from the former.

I like these kinds of stories, and I was lucky enough to be allowed to take some plants away with me.

◀ 'Catalogna' is an Italian lettuce variety with long, slender leaves. It was sown directly in a bed in early May. The salad leaves are ready for harvest in early July—leave them too long, and the lettuce will bolt and start to bloom.

▲ 'Kew Rambler' is an incredibly lush and vibrant climbing rose that can be grown up a fruit tree (see pages 234–235). Here, Hilde has stretched the shoots horizontally along the chestnut fence (see page 275). It has small, pinkish-white single flowers, followed in autumn by beautiful orange rosehips.

▶ 'Belle de Rémalard' is yet another climbing rose. It was planted last year and is only just beginning to catch on. Once that happens, it can easily stretch to 3 or 4 feet (about 1 m). The flowers are pink and half-double. Over time, it will also grow along the chestnut fence.

▲ 'Carthusian Pink' (*Dianthus carthusianorum*) is an elegant, single-flowered pink carnation with slender, erect stems—not a perennial you see often.

▶ Another carnation, 'Sweet William' (*Dianthus barbatus*). This is usually sold as part of mixed seed packs, but if you are particularly keen on a specific color variant, they can be propagated from cuttings. Working from seeds, it is far from certain that the color will be the same as the flower from which the seeds were harvested. However, there are a few named varieties for which you can buy seeds: dark red 'Sooty', pink 'Noverna Purple', white 'Albus', and the purple/white 'Purple Crown'.

▼ Bellflower (*Campanula persicifolia*) 'Alba' self-seeds in many places in the kitchen garden—and is most welcome to do so!

◄ I think we can all agree that it is wonderful to pick a bouquet of sweet peas (*Lathyrus odoratus*), put them in a small vase, and enjoy their scent. Few flowers have such a lovely fragrance, hence the Latin name.

► Ground elder is generally unwelcome in gardens, but it's actually quite beautiful when in bloom. It adds a uniquely distinctive character to a bouquet of roses, for example, as a complement to the pink climbing rose 'Alexandre Girault' seen here or the creamy white 'Goldfinch' at the top. The latter is an old variety that first saw the light of day in 1907. It can grow up to 9 to 12 feet (3 to 4 m) high and 6 feet (2 m) wide. Up against a fruit tree is an ideal spot.

◄ 'Rosa Mundi', with its candy-colored petals, is unique. It has beautiful rosehips in late summer.

► Once you see its shapely flowers, it's obvious why the rose 'Raubritter' has so many fans. In theory, it is supposed to grow to about 6 feet (2 m), but that has never been the case in my garden.

◀ Most of the roses in Hilde's garden are old heirloom varieties that only bloom once per season, all the more reason to enjoy them while you can ('Reine des Violettes' is in the middle of the photo).

▼ Your nose will detect the regal lily (*Lilium regale*) from yards away.

▲ The profusion of white roses in the middle is remarkably impressive. These are two roses growing in beautiful union over a portal-like construction at the entrance to the garden (see the large picture on page 278)–'Félicité et Perpétue' and the rambling *Rosa helenae*. The latter was bred in Denmark in 1930 by Aksel Olsen.

▶ The garden contains many delphiniums, which need support to stop them from falling over. Hilde bought this blue flower under the name 'Berghimmel', but we both agree that 'Berghimmel' is a much lighter blue. She must have been sent the wrong variety.

Pure Cottage Style   305

▲ It is truly impressive that the family thatches their own roof. Raymund and two of their sons who live at home spent much of summer 2018 doing it. The roses are the same as in the picture on page 301—pink 'Alexandre Girault' and creamy-white 'Goldfinch'.

◀ Barrels collect rainwater at several spots in the garden. This one was a gift.

▲ An idyllic spot for an open-air nap. To the left is 'Guirlande d'Amour' (white), in the middle 'Centenaire de Lourdes' (pink), and in the background 'Laguna' (pink). 'Centenaire de Lourdes' is a shrub, while the other two are climbing roses. It's a bit difficult to see here because the long shoots from 'Guirlande d'Amour' disappear out of frame to the left, while 'Laguna' grows up into the shrub behind.

▶ I'm sure most people have been given an unnamed plant as a gift. That's the case with this rose. The person who gave it to Hilde didn't know what it was called. She had grown it from a cutting and just thought it was pretty. There is no doubting its loveliness, but it would have been nice for Hilde to know the name, as visitors sometimes ask.

▲ Another impressive group of delphiniums. This type, called 'Ouvertüre', has a soft blue color, best described as swimming-pool blue. After flowering, Hilde cuts them all the way down. They then flower again in August, although the plants don't grow as tall.

◄ Clary sage (*Salvia sclarea*) is a very beautiful but not very common biennial. It has an absolutely fantastic play of colors, which shimmer between pink and blue. If you place it alongside blue flowers, it seems to mirror them, and the same is true with pink flowers.

This particular sage grows well over 1 yard (1 m) tall and almost as wide. In my garden, we often cut the stalk when it reaches 12 to 16 inches (30 to 40 cm). After that, it grows several new stalks that reach about 2 foot 8 inches (80 cm).

The plant in the background is Macedonian scabious (*Knautia macedonica*).

▲The pink rose in the middle of the picture is 'Mme. Isaac Pereire'. Ever since it first arrived on the market in 1881, it has been loved and admired for its attractive flowers and enchanting fragrance. Some even call it the most beautiful rose scent ever!

People sometimes ask me which season I like best. It's hard because I love them all! My motto is that there is always something to look forward to. But if I absolutely had to answer, I would say high summer, when all the roses are in bloom. During the long, balmy evenings, I sometimes have to pinch myself while walking around the garden because it seems like some kind of wonderful dream. It's a particularly fabulous time.

▶ The giant bellflower (*Campanula latifolia* var. *macrantha*) 'Alba' is a fairly easy perennial. It is reasonably undemanding in terms of habitat and copes well with both partial shade and full sun. It quickly forms a relatively large group and mixes well with roses.

◄ It's truly magical to see a rose cover the crown of an old apple tree—in this case, 'Paul's Himalayan Musk'. This impressive climbing rose with small, full pink flowers can grow up to about 19 feet (6 m) tall. The scent is almost intoxicating. It was first mentioned in the nineteenth century but not registered until 1915.

▼ Cohosh bugbane (*Cimicifuga racemosa*) is a stately perennial with upright stems that reveal its white flowers in August and smells lovely.

▲ Hilde has also planted ornamental grasses in the beds. Golden oats (*Stipa gigantea*) is always recognizable by its distinctive sun-catching seedheads, which look almost golden. This is a perennial that comes back year after year.

▶ There are also annual grasses, such as foxtail barley (*Hordeum jubatum*), seen here nestled among some lavender. It happily self-seeds in many places, but given the light-colored heads, it's hard to imagine a place where it wouldn't be a great fit!

◀ The genus *Nepeta* includes several species, such as catnip (*Nepeta kubanica*).

▶ Hilde has *Phacelia esculentum* in the garden, mainly for the benefit of useful insects who are attracted to the sweet, honey-like scent. She knows from experience that sowing Phacelia between rows of vegetables reduces aphid infestations.

◀ In terms of cottage gardens, it simply doesn't get any better than this. The adorable play of colors is the kind of sublime beauty that only nature can conjure up.

▼ Whenever I see a field of red poppies (*Papaver rhoeas*), I have to stop and admire them. But fields like that are becoming increasingly rare. Maybe it's just that fewer fields are left fallow these days.

▲ Few other plants look as graceful as fennel in bloom. The lime-yellow inflorescences also look good in bouquets.

▼ Borage or starflower (*Borago officinalis*) in the company of pot marigold (*Calendula*). Pot marigold is one of the easiest summer flowers to grow. Let it self-seed, and it's guaranteed to return the following year.

▲ As the name suggests, the everlasting pea is a perennial that returns time after time. Not having to bother sowing every year sounds very enticing, of course, but the everlasting pea has one big downside—it has no scent. Nor does it come in all the characteristically endearing colors of the annual sweet pea (*Lathyrus odoratus*). Having said that, the everlasting version is pretty easy to grow and long-lived. This variety is called 'Pink Pearl'.

▼ 'Belle de Rémalard' is one of the garden's many pink roses and reliably produces a lot of flowers.

▲ The flowers under the arch include golden marguerite (*Anthemis tinctoria*), which some people call a weed. Hilde values it highly. In the olden days, the plant was used for dyeing textiles. Also pictured are ox-eye daisy (*Leucanthemum vulgare*) and pot marigold (*Calendula*).

▲ The tractor in the background is a reminder that this is in fact a working farm. Unfortunately, there are fewer and fewer of them as agriculture becomes increasingly industrialized. I fondly remember the gardens of my grandparents and their siblings in West Jutland. We rarely had dinner there but would often join them for evening coffee. Most were farmers and had milking to do. After coffee, the men went into the stable, the women and children into the garden. It was a tradition. I vividly remember being fascinated by the colorful beds. This was probably when the seeds for my love of gardening were planted.

▶ A wonderful memento of the family's cars over the years. The garden tools are not just for decoration, though.

▲ The late-flowering clematis (*Clematis viticella*) 'Rubra', has the most beautiful reddish-purple flowers. Like all viticella species, it blooms fairly late in the season and has to be cut back before spring. It will then shoot up again to a height of a few meters before the buds appear.

◄ A yellow marigold (*Calendula*) shining like a little sun.

► A wonderful symbiosis. The golden marguerite (*Anthemis tinctoria*) and the white ox-eye daisy (*Leucanthemum vulgare*) are quite similar in shape. Both capture the wild spirit of the garden.

▲ Perennial clematis (*Clematis integrifolia*) 'Pamiat Serdtsa' does not climb or wind its way up. Rather, its erect, slightly stiff stems need support. In the large photograph on the previous page, it is growing up a support in the background and to the right. Hilde has a penchant for the small-flowering clematis, which is nowhere near as demanding as its larger cousins. On the whole, she likes discreet plants.

▶ Nettle-leaved mullein (*Verbascum chaixii*) 'Yellow' grows to around 3 feet (1 m), making it a medium-height variety. Some grow up to two or three times as big, while others reach just 12 to 16 inches (30 to 40 cm). The lemon-yellow color really stands out. The white *Verbascum chaixii* 'Album' (see page 323) is more common than the yellow version.

▼ These days, I rarely encounter flowers I've never seen before, but hoary alyssum (*Berteroa incana*) was new to me. It is always great to learn something new. This is a lovely little plant that also grows in the wild.

▼ It's not only the flowers that get bigger with each visit—the lambs do too.

◀ Double yellow, *Verbascum chaixii* 'Yellow' and *Anthemis tinctoria*. This is such a cheerful, optimistic color. Fortunately, Hilde also likes yellow.

◀ ▲ Pot marigolds, a wonderful sight for both humans and the bees found everywhere in the kitchen garden. Hilde is very aware of the need for bee-friendly flowers—that's one reason why she has so many poppies. The pot marigolds interbreed, so you get both orange and yellow varieties and different shapes.

◀ This delicate, light-yellow sunflower, called 'Italian White', only grows about 5 feet (1.5 m) tall. This means that it can stand on its own without support. In summer, it attracts bees and in the fall, birds.

▲ ◀ *Clematis viticella*, 'Madame Julia Correvon' is one of the best-known clematis varieties. It is highly prized because it flowers so readily and so vigorously, as the pictures clearly show. In the background is Fuller's teasel (*Dipsacus sativus*), the thistle-like look of which makes it ideal for a wild garden. And, at over 6 feet (2 m) tall, it's definitely a plant people notice!

▶ *Commelina tuberosa* is a lovely little plant, standing 10 to 12 inches (25 to 30 cm). It's a short-lived perennial that will only last a couple of seasons. But in a good spot, it will self-seed so often that you won't notice that it's somewhat transitory.

▶ Purple toadflax (*Linaria purpurea*) 'Canon J. Went' is a slender, self-seeding plant that pops up all over the beds. This is a discreet species that grows to a height of around 2.5 feet (70 to 80 cm) and fits in everywhere.

▲ The pink phlox (*Phlox amplifolia*) 'Apanatschi' is slightly shorter and more slender than the common garden phlox (*Phlox paniculata*). Otherwise, the two species are very similar, and it can be difficult to spot the difference.

▶ Here, again, is catnip (*Nepeta kubanica*), with its beautiful lavender-blue flowers. There are various different species of catnip, which is part of the mint family. The best known is *Nepeta faassenii* 'Six Hills Giant', which is not quite as upright as this one. Catnip is so named because cats love it and will happily roll around in it. Hilde avoids that by covering it with netting.

◀ The cotton thistle, *Onopordum acanthium*, grows to around 6 feet (2 m) tall. It is notable for its silver-gray foliage and beautiful flowers. It is also called the Scottish thistle, as it is the national flower of Scotland.

▶ Yellow ox-eye (*Telekia speciosa*) also reaches about 6 feet (2 m) in height. This is a true late-summer perennial.

◀ Although I am reasonably strict when it comes to color schemes and like a bed with harmonious tones, I was pretty excited about this one, which is very much as nature intended. I would never have even thought of planting bright-red flowers along with pink.

▶ Montbretia (*Crocosmia*) 'Lucifer' is an optimistic bright-red flower guaranteed to make you smile. At about 3 feet (1 m), it is the tallest montbretia.

◀ On page 317, we saw *Verbascum chaixii* 'Yellow'. Here is the white version, 'Album'.

▼ Purple loosestrife (*Lythrum salicaria*) has upright stems that peek up over the other perennials

▲ My final visit to Ibba Garten is at the end of August. Late summer has just set in, and the golden hop (*Humulus lupulus*) 'Aureus' has reached the very top of the arch. Many of the vegetables have already been harvested, but there are still plants in the greenhouse waiting to be moved outdoors. This is intensive cultivation, in a good way.

◀ When the bulb tops start to crack, it's harvest time. Dig up the bulbs and lay or hang them out to dry. This is very important to make sure they last the winter, which is the general idea, of course.

▲ The soil is ready for another batch of crops, such as lettuce, spinach, and radish. Some beetroot seeds were sown in trays a few weeks ago, with small spaces between them, and are now ready for planting out. The garden is beautiful, but some flowers are, of course, fading. For example, montbretia (*Crocosmia*) 'Lucifer' still has sporadic flowers, but soon only the seedheads will remain. These are very decorative and look good in bouquets.

▶ Rows of beautiful lettuces. It has been incredibly educational to follow the kitchen garden over an entire season.

▲ There's something fascinating about winter pumpkins. The plants crawl upwards into the air instead of covering the ground. It's a solution that's both practical and beautiful. Pumpkins hanging like this sometimes grow so heavy that the stem breaks. Before that happens, it's a good idea to support them with nets, as you might with cantaloupes.

◀ This variety, called 'Futsu Black', is native to Japan. In late summer, the pumpkin changes color from greenish black (like here) to somewhere between beige and cinnamon-colored. It's such a beautiful vegetable! It is important that the pumpkin matures completely on the plant. After that, it can last up to half a year. It has a very subtle flavor.

The vast majority of pumpkins are orange, but they come in other colors too. A popular yellow variety is 'Mellow Yellow', which ripens pretty early and can be used in the same way as a squash. In the past, pumpkins were often grown on a compost heap. This is a good idea in that it usually yields large pumpkins, but it also drains nutrients from the compost.

The cabbages—in the foreground, palm kale—have not finished growing yet. As long as the weather remains warm, they will continue to grow. It is said that it is best to wait until there is frost before harvesting palm and curly kale. Any plants that the family doesn't eat are left where they are until spring, when they begin to bloom and then later seed. The light-yellow flowers are beautiful in a salad.

◀ Hollyhocks and
an old farmhouse
with half-timbering
and thatched roof.
It doesn't get much
better than this. When
Hilde has time, she
goes around the garden
and cuts off the round
seedheads. If she
does it early enough,
new buds and another
bunch of flowers
will emerge.

▼ Tansy (*Tanacetum*)
resembles a daisy,
only without the
white petals. This is
a low-maintenance
plant that grows freely
both in the garden
and along ditches
from late summer
to early autumn.

▲ Globe thistle (*Echinops ritro*) is a gorgeous late-summer perennial with decorative spherical inflorescences. *Echinus* is Latin for sea urchin. The white flowers seen sporadically between the blue spheres are white goat rams (*Epilobium angustifolium*) 'Album.'

▶ In a bouquet, thistle heads are nicely complemented by umbels, like the toothpick plant (*Ammi visnaga*), a lovely, almost lace-like summer flower.

Index